Collection Development and Public Access of Government Documents

PROCEEDINGS OF
THE FIRST ANNUAL
LIBRARY GOVERNMENT DOCUMENTS
AND INFORMATION CONFERENCE

Collection Development and Public Access of Government Documents

PROCEEDINGS OF
THE FIRST ANNUAL
LIBRARY GOVERNMENT DOCUMENTS
AND INFORMATION CONFERENCE

Edited by Peter Hernon
Graduate School of Library and
Information Science
Simmons College, Boston

MECKLER PUBLISHING
520 Riverside Ave., Westport, CT 06880
3 Henrietta Street, London WC2E 8LU, England

Library of Congress Cataloging in Publication Data

Library Government Documents and Information
      Conference (1st : 1981 : Boston, Mass.)
      Collection development and public access of
government documents.

      Held in Boston, Mass., Mar. 3-4, 1981.
      Bibliography: p.
      1. Government publications—Library resources
—United States—Congresses.   2. Libraries—
United States—Special Collections—Government
publications—Congresses.   I. Hernon, Peter.
II. Title.
Z7164.G7L5   1982   [Z1223.Z7]   025.17'34   82-3435
ISBN 0-930466-49-7   AACR2

CONTENTS

TABLES

FIGURES

PREFACE

The articles in this book are based on presentations delivered at the first Annual Library Government Documents and Information Conference sponsored by *Microform Review Inc.* and held in Boston on March 3 and 4, 1981. This conference program, as well as future ones, provides a fresh perspective to the documents field and addresses issues not well-developed in the published literature. More specifically, the programs encourage discussion of documents librarianship in the 1980s, agency publishing practices and distribution services for the decade, theoretical and philosophical issues, as well as a number of research projects. The conferences clearly demonstrate the need for better balance in the documents field between theory and practice, with each furthering the development of the other. Research, alone, may not solve all problems or abate disagreement, but it will significantly add to existing knowledge, clarify issues, place opinions and assumptions in proper perspective, and create an awareness of unforeseen areas which merit further investigation.

Papers for the first conference focused on two themes: public access to government publications and collection development. Bernard M. Fry sees the need for a theory based on principles and standards as essential for the further development of government publication handling. In order to provide effective access to government publications, librarians, he believes, should be aggressive in their relationship with all user groups.

LeRoy C. Schwarzkopf provides an historical overview of public access to the depository library program operated by the U.S. Government Printing Office. As he points out, the federal government does not regard the program as a major means for public access to government publications. Charles R. McClure maintains that the GPO depository program needs formal evaluation based on an analysis of appropriate goals and objectives. He identifies critical assumptions underlying the program and stresses the need for clear performance measures to determine the adequacy of the system and as a means to suggest alternative depository structures. Incorporating features from several different structures, McClure presents the model which he regards as most feasible. Joe Morehead examines users of government publications and questions the reliability of government generated statistics. In this regard, he asks a very important question: what is the role of librarians in the provision of such information to unsophisticated users? Are librarians merely collectors, organizers, and retrievers of information, or should they perform an advocacy role? William J. Barrett, who provides an overview of the GPO in the 1980s, hypothesizes that further applications of technology will make a profound impact on the delivery and packaging of information. In his opinion, the type of government publications contained in libraries will change as the paperless society approaches and as publishing in paper form becomes even less economical.

Collection development represents a topic of increasing concern to libraries, especially with the proliferation of government information generated each year and with many libraries facing zero growth for document collections. Greater emphasis on selective acquisition and weeding is necessary in order to avoid congestion in processing, storage, and servicing. Luciana Marulli-Koenig examines collection development for United Nations documents. She focuses on collection development policies and principles, the scope of collecting, acquisition methods, selection tools, and weeding. Peter I. Hajnal, who discusses bibliographic control of Unesco publications and documents, identifies appropriate bibliographic tools and notes the types of Unesco source material most likely to be used. The final two articles are based on research in progress. The first one, by Peter Hernon and Gary R. Purcell, discusses selection patterns for depository libraries as represented in the GPO automated list of item numbers. As the authors note, the file is currently of limited value for collection development analyses because the item numbers do not convey a subject orientation. Such an emphasis needs to be placed on the item file. The other article, by Peter Hernon and Clayton Shepherd, characterizes the government publications represented in the 1979 *Social Sciences Citation Index*. Knowledge of the types and titles of government publications cited by social scientist can be useful to librarians in making selection and retention decisions.

The conference and these proceedings represent an attempt to stimulate thinking and writing in the documents field. Documents librarianship contains an extensive body of literature. Yet, many of these writings are provincial and redundant, fulfilling a service function or conveying a particular viewpoint. A need clearly exists for increased production of research related to government publications, the introduction of innovative approaches to resolve ongoing problems, and more critical evaluation of underlying assumptions. We must all work together to move the documents literature in new directions and to minimize duplication of effort. It is my hope that the annual conference and these proceedings make a contribution in this regard.

Peter Hernon
Simmons College
May 1981

THE NEED FOR A THEORETICAL BASE

By Bernard M. Fry

It is widely accepted that government publications constitute a unique body of literature,—undervalued and underutilized—which is both a part of the official record of government and also a primary source of authoritative and up-to-date information for the public. Because of their official and unique character, and the current trend to a primary commitment to users, in terms of objectives and in terms of service, government publications today represent a significant and integral part of the national information resources.

Document librarianship is a dynamic, growing, and purposeful enterprise. To be sure, there are financial, staffing, and space problems too large to ignore, but despite such constraints, we have, individually and collectively, an opportunity to test our capabilities and to expand our horizons in a field which continues to grow in importance each year. It is in this context I wish to discuss "the need for a theoretical base."

Since this inquiry is broadly aimed, it will undertake not to preempt other chapters of this book; in particular, detailed examination of problem areas affected by the neglect of theory will be kept to a minimum. Major components in the government documents/information communications cycle—publication, distribution, and access—will be treated only in so far as they relate to the development of a common body of theory.

NEGLECT OF THEORY

Over the past fifty years document librarians have evolved efficient systems of practice, but they have failed to formulate a corresponding system of theory to guide, justify, and control that practice. There has been neglect of theory which would provide a setting to which document handling practice could be related and against which the effectiveness and efficiency of that practice might be measured. Most of the contemporary methods of document librarianship have been based on ad hoc assumptions related to conventional library materials, in the absence of well-established theory of document availability and access.

Almost without exception, library handling of government documents/information has developed through a cumulation of immediate empirical procedures, with little planning or looking very far ahead either in techniques or technology. If it has touched upon theory at all it has worked backward from practice. Theory followed practice instead of leading it. Neglect in the development of theory as an underpinning and validation of practice has prevented a clear determination of goals and objectives and implementation of measures to achieve them.

The neglect of theory in librarianship may be partly explained in historical terms. Fifty years ago Pierce Butler charged that though librarians "know very well how to do things," they "have only vague notions of why they do them." They have, he admitted, evolved "highly efficient systems of practice," but they have failed to formulate "a corresponding system of theory to elucidate, justify, and control of that practice."[1] Over the years similar criticism of the profession has been made by many others who contend that we "have not yet succeeded in establishing our professional purpose."

Well-established theory is needed to provide a setting to which practice could be related and against which the effectiveness of that practice might be measured. To return to Butler's phrase, a theory tells librarians not how to do things, but why such things should be done. Theory, then, is not antithetical to practice; on the contrary, the two are natural allies.

Librarians today need more than ever to formulate a theoretical structure of their function based on sound principles and standards. There are unmistakable changes taking place in librarianship that may well reshape the library before the end of this century.

NEW MISSION AND REORGANIZATION

Implications for research in the context of a new statement of mission for library depositories, that is, to emphasize communications, and not only documents/information retrieval, are numerous and far-reaching. Perhaps the major area for inquiry would involve organization adjustments, including a system-as-a-whole approach involving all levels of government, federal, state, and local. This goal could be achieved without radical change. The building blocks are at hand. A few states have already moved in the direction of incorporating bibliographic control of local documents with state documents and state depositories. At least fifteen of the present Federal regional depositories are administered by state libraries. It would not be difficult to establish an overall cost effective system, including also Federal Information Centers,—a step recommended by the White House Conference and later endorsed by President Carter to Congress—at least on a pilot basis of three to five centers.[2]

The mechanism and precedents for funding are in place. Evidence of this is the fact that Patent Office depositories, which are already selective depositories, are minimally funded as are Federal Information Centers. The logic for funding, perhaps sponsored by the Intergovernmental Relations Commitee, can be reinforced by proof of economy (e.g., eliminating waste and duplication at present widespread among and within different levels of government) and also overall improvement in effective communication between governments and the public.

Organization re-alignment would perhaps bring significant results, if re-inforced by the adoption of a new conceptual theory of communication, with emphasis on information transfer as well as information retrieval.

Physical availability on the shelf or in reasonable proximity, coupled with adequate bibliographic apparatus, constitutes access in the broadest sense. In this age of maximum media exposure the documents librarian cannot rely on assurance of public availability and access. Collectively and individually librarians must undertake innovative measures, in co-operation with other concerned institutions and agencies, to provide guides to content analysis. Such guides could take the form of information analysis products similar to those produced by ERIC and its Clearinghouses. The latter provide an essential filtering function according to subject areas. They act as delegated agents to review and separate out the trivial, duplicative and non-substantive. A parallel is also found in the development of Information Analysis Centers, similar to those funded by the Federal government for scientific and technical fields (about sixty). In the realm of national policies and issues of pressing interest, for example, primary source materials would draw heavily upon government publications for authoritative and up-to-date information, objectively filtered and reviewed by issuing agencies and offices to provide maximum potential for information transfer to the public, in the past overwhelmed by multi-media and a flood of unevaluated documents.

GOVERNMENT PUBLICATIONS AS INFORMATION RESOURCES

The success or failure in the development of conceptually significant theory of document library services will determine in large measure whether government publications become an active and useful channel of government communication to the public. The still accelerating numbers of publications issued at all levels of government make the task of formulating a consensus theory of services all the more pressing and urgent.

As a means to this end, it is useful to review the evolutionary stages of government publications as information resources:

- Official records: storage and retrieval by source
- Document identification and delivery
- Document and information storage and retrieval
- Bibliographic data bases with retrieval by subject headings and identifiers
- Document content retrieval and analysis
- Information analysis across all types and levels of official publications
- Development of knowledge base programs which filter, evaluate, and distill knowledge derived from the range of library materials including government publications. Government publications, because of their unique role in providing authoritative and up-to-date information, will frequently form the "cutting edge" of efforts to communicate among specialists and between government and the public.

It is widely accepted today that government publications are undervalued and underutilized as information resources. Several steps are essential to bring government publications into the mainstream of information resources which serve as the basic building materials for knowledge base programs:

- Matrix selection by subject as well as by SuDocs number
- Improvement in format and organization of publications issued or sponsored by government. This should extend to normal reading aids such as abstracts, indexes, readability, etc.
- Filtering by issuing agencies to eliminate the strictly administrative, trivial, duplicative, or superseded.
- Aids, i.e., information analysis products, knowledge base programs, information clusters, compilations of information from all sources and in all formats, e.g., the Pathfinder series, etc.

There is growing evidence that existing perceptions of government documents as a supportive library service should be upgraded in concept and in practice to meet the needs of members of our increasingly pluralistic and complex society. Because of growing political consciousness and the new Federalism, combined with the interdependence of all levels of government, government publications/information need to play an increasing role in government communication to the public. As this trend accelerates, it will be incumbent upon the library profession to expand its preparation not only with respect to technological innovations, but also with respect to its ability to organize, structure, and communicate information in an educationally sound manner.

To paraphrase the aphorism characterizing the railroad industry—its business is transportation. The central concern of document librarians is the communication of government publications/information and is not limited to making document handling services more efficient? The simplified distinction, of course, is not clear cut but is a matter of emphasis. Document services without express attention to their central purpose of communication would result in a sterile and non-productive effort, and likely rejection by the public.

Politically as well as financially, it is essential that we sever the umbilical cord and break dramatically with the passive image of our archival heritage. Such action will serve to improve the present state of low priority with respect to allocation of limited library resources. A prerequisite is that our role in the communication of government publications/information to the public be acknowledged by the Federal government, as has already been done in the case of support for Federal Information Centers and Patent depositories.

Daniel Bell,[3] Peter Drucker[4] and others have hailed the coming of the post-industrial society in which knowledge would replace capital and industry as society's most important resource. This new conception, questioned by some, has focused on the supreme importance of electronics information systems and services. The gathering and transmitting of vast amounts of unfiltered and unevaluated information and raw data is technically feasible today, but its assembling or transformation into knowledge useful and used by the public is another matter altogether.

The central question for libraries, information managers and other gatekeepers is not whether libraries will wither in the face of electronics alternatives, but whether we will recognize and act upon our professional opportunities to meet the public need. To this end consensus on a sound theoretical base is essential.

REFERENCES

1. Pierce Butler. *Introduction to Library Science*. Chicago: University of Chicago Press, 1961.

2. "President Carter's Message on Libraries and Information," *Library Journal*, 105 (November 1, 1980): 2278-2279.

3. Daniel Bell. *The Coming of Post-Industrial Society*. New York: Basic Books, 1973.

4. Various writings by Peter Drucker are pertinent. For example, see Peter Drucker. *Technology, Management and Society*. New York: Harper and Row, 1973.

DEPOSITORY LIBRARIES AND PUBLIC ACCESS

By LeRoy C. Schwarzkopf

What is the basic job of the depository library system? In early 1974, Bernadine Hoduski, now an influential staff member of the Joint Committee on Printing but then a librarian at the EPA Seventh Region in Kansas City, asked this question in the title of an article in the *Drexel Library Quarterly*. Citing section 1911 of Title 44, *U.S. Code*, she answered that "the basic job of the federal depository library system is to make 'government publications available for the free use of the general public'."[1] She also linked this basic job primarily with those libraries that obtained their depository status through a Congressional designation particularly from a Representative, and whose immediate responsibility should be directed to a Congressional district. However, she failed to ask what is the purpose of those libraries which obtained their status through other than designation by a Congressman, and have "by law" designations. The "by law" designations include state libraries, highest state appellate court libraries, federal libraries, land grant college libraries, and accredited law school libraries.

In 1977, this author prepared a paper on behalf of the American Library Association and its Government Documents Round Table for presentation at the meeting of the IFLA Section on Official Publications, 1977 World Congress of Librarians. Published in *Government Publications Review*, it carried a statement similar to Ms. Hoduski and based on the statutory language in section 1911: "The basic purpose of the depository library program is to provide reference collections of official publications in the 435 congressional districts of the 50 states and in the outlying territories of the United States, where they will be accessible free of charge to the public."[2]

However, this author continued with the following statement: "This worthy purpose which depository librarians accept (perhaps now amended to be "accept as gospel") is nowhere strongly stated in the legal history." Indeed, the legislative history of Title 44 indicates that section 1911 with the "free use" clause was inserted to establish one of the conditions that libraries must satisfy to retain their depository status, and not as a statement of the basic purpose of the program. The depository library program is primarily a library initiated program for the benefit of participating libraries. Changes have usually resulted from initiatives from the library community, and not from the federal government, and particularly not from the Government Printing Office (GPO) which has the prime responsibility for the operation of the program. GPO has traditionally looked to the library community to study and research the program and to initiate changes, and it has generally acted to improve the program administratively only when pressured to do so by the library community (and not by the public, or other elements of the federal government.)

The purpose of this article is to take an impartial, rather than a partisan view of the legislative history of the depository library system. This review of the historical background attempts to provide an objective basis for an analysis and improvement of the program. No specific recommendations for improvement will be offered, since Charles R. McClure makes recommendations for a restructured depository library system in these proceedings. It should be noted that the program has through its long history provided public access (though not as widely as it probably could, or should) to a growing amount and diversity of government publications and information.

In tracing the legislative history of the depository library program, the best - and usual - starting point is the introduction in the annual committee print published by the Joint Committee on Printing, *Government Depository Libraries: the Present Law Governing Designated Depository Libraries*. This document presents an excellent brief historical background and provides citations for major landmark legislation. Another way is to start with the Depository Library Act of 1962 (Public Law 87-579, approved August 9, 1962, 76 *Stat.* 352) which provides citations back to the Printing Act of 1895 and to the *Revised Statutes* of 1873-74. These two in turn, especially the *Revised Statutes*, provide references and citations to earlier legislation.

The depository library system had its origins in special acts of the first twelve Congresses which provided for the printing of extra copies of Congressional documents for distribution outside the federal government to the states and territories. In the Thirteenth Congress, Joint Resolution 1 of December 27, 1813 (3 *Stat.* 140) provided

that of the public journals of the Senate and of the House of Representatives, *of the present and every future congress*, commencing with the present session, and of the documents published under the orders of the Senate and of the House of Representatives respectively, from the commencement of the present session, there shall be printed two hundred copies beyond the usual number...and shall be transmitted, to the executives of the several states and territories, as shall be sufficient to furnish one copy to each executive, one copy to each branch of every state and territorial legislature, one copy to each university and college in each state, and one copy to the Historical Society...in each state.

The number of extra copies was increased from 200 to 250 by Joint Resolution no. 5 of July 20, 1840 (5 *Stat.* 409) and to 300 by Joint Resolution no. 5 of April 30, 1844 (5 *Stat.* 717).

The depository library program was formally established by a series of two resolutions in 1857 and 1858 and an Act of 1859. Resolution no. 5 of January 28, 1857 (11 *Stat.* 253) transferred responsibility for distribution of the journals and documents from the Department of State to the Department of the Interior. It also provided that

so many of the 400 copies of the public documents...as are now distributed by the Department of State to colleges and other literary institutions, shall be deposited with the Secretary of the Interior, for distribution to such colleges, public libraries, athenaeums, literary and scientific institutions, boards of trade, or public associations as may be designated by him.

Despite this lengthy list of eligible recipients most of the depositories were libraries. However, the Boston Athenaeum is still a depository; the JCP committee print lists its date of designation by a Representative as unknown. The 1857 resolution was amended by Joint Resolution no. 5 of March 20, 1858 (11 *Stat.* 368) which provided that the designations would be made by "the representative in Congress from each congressional district, and by the delegate from each Territory in the United States."

The 1858 Resolution was in turn amended by section 5 of an Act of February 5, 1859 (11*Stat.* 380) which provided that designations would be made by "each of the senators from the several States, respectively, and by the representative in Congress from each congressional district, and by the delegate from each Territory in the United States." The principle of congressional designation as the basis for the depository library system was thus established, with an apparent intent to provide distribution on an equal basis throughout the country. Another provision of Section 5 provides distribution of Congressional journals and documents "to the governors of the States and Territories." Although it is not specifically stated, the statutory language implies that each Senator, Representative, and Delegate could make only one designation. Section 10 of the 1859 Act also introduced a requirement for permanent retention as one of the provisions for accepting such materials in the following language: "all documents as provided by law, shall be kept there and not removed from such place."

The first evidence of an inspection authority for the supervisor of the depository program will be found in Section 2 of the Act of March 2, 1861 (12 *Stat*. 245) which provided that "in the future the public documents to be distributed by the Secretary of the Interior shall be sent to the institutions already designated, unless he shall be satisfied that any such institution is no longer a suitable depository of the same."

An Act of March 3, 1869 (15 *Stat*. 292) established a position of Superintendent of Public Documents in the Department of the Interior with the responsibility for distributing public documents to depository libraries, and to other officials and institutions authorized by law. The laws relating to the duties and responsibilities of the Superintendent of Public Documents were codified by the *Revised Statutes* of 1873-74 in Chapter 7, sections 497-511. The acts and resolutions mentioned above were codified primarily in sections 501 and 502, but also in sections 503 and 504. Indeed, most of sections 501 and 502 remained in effect until repealed by the Depository Library Act of 1962. Apparently the law as codified in Title 44 prior to 1962 was never passed as a separate act for approval by the President. Section 502 of the *Revised Statutes* also contains a provision whose origin this author was unable to trace: i.e., "that the journals and public documents shall be sent only to designated depositories as shall signify a willingness to pay the cost of their transportation." This requirement to pay postage was eliminated by the Depository Library Act of 1962. It was considered an unnecessary administrative burden to the depositories, and it represented only a small cost of the program to the government.

The Printing Act of 1895 approved January 12, 1895 (28 *Stat*. 601) had as its main object the consolidation of existing laws on the printing, binding, and distribution of public documents. Provisions affecting the depository library program are scattered throughout the 100 sections of this 24 page law. With respect to public access, its primary effect was to increase the categories of materials which were distributed to depository libraries.

Probably of equal, or greater, significance for public access was the establishment of a systematic program for the bibliographic control of government documents. The depository library program has since been closely related to, and significantly affected by bibliographic control programs.

There is no one section in the 1895 Act which lists all the types of materials which should be distributed to depository libraries. Depository distribution is authorized in various sections of the Act pertaining to particular types or specific titles of documents, and depository distribution is included with other distribution formulae provided by law for that category or title.

In Section 54 covering distribution of unbound and bound House and Senate Documents and Reports, five hundred copies of the bound documents and reports only (i.e. Congressional Serial Set volumes) were allotted to "the superintendent of documents...for distribution to the State and Territorial libraries *and* designated depositories." Thus depository libraries would continue to receive Congressional documents, but only in the bound Serial Set. Since depositories did not receive the unbound reports and documents, this resulted in significant delays in receipt of reports on bills which are critical elements in tracing legislation.

At this point, several developments about the 1895 Act inherent in Section 54 (as well as in other sections) of the Act should be mentioned. The office of the Superintendent of Public Documents, formerly in the Department of the Interior was transferred to the Government Printing Office and renamed "Superintendent of Documents." The Superintendent of Documents was assigned responsibility for the new three element bibliographic control system established by the Act.

(1) Section 62 required him to prepare at the end of each regular session of Congress "a comprehensive index of public documents" to include "every document printed by the Government Printing Office... (and)...every document issued or published by such (Executive) Department, bureau or office not confidential in character." This became the *Catalogue of Public Documents of the Congress and of All Departments of the Government of the United States*, usually called the *Document Catalogue* which was published from 1895 to 1947 covering the period 1893 through 1940. In 1947 the Joint Committee on Printing ruled that the *Monthly Catalog* satisfied the provisions of Section 62, and the *Document Catalogue* was discontinued.

(2) Section 62 also authorized a "consolidated index of Congressional Documents." This became the annual *Index to Reports and Documents of Congress*, usually called the *Document Index* which was published from 1895 to 1933 when it was superseded by the *Numerical Lists and Schedules of*

Volumes of the Reports and Documents of Congress. The *Numerical List* will be discontinued with the 96th Congress and incorporated into the *Monthly Catalog.*

(3) Section 69 directed that a "Catalog of Government publications shall be prepared by the Superintendent of Documents on the first day of each month which shall show the documents printed during the preceeding month, where obtainable, and the price thereof." This became the familiar *Monthly Catalog of United States Government Publications,* popularly called the *Monthly Catalog,* which has been published since 1895. The Superintendent of Documents was also assigned responsibility for the sale of public documents. Thus, there was combined in one agency (the Government Printing Office) responsibility for the printing, distribution, sale, and bibliographic control of U.S. government documents. This has played a significant role in the evolution of the depository library system, and of public access to government publications and information.

Another significant part of Section 54, and other sections pertaining to depository distribution, was that the following statutory language was used: "State and territorial libraries *and* designated depositories." Indeed, the Depository Library Act of 1962 and its subsequent codification in Chapter 19, Title 44 continues to use similar language: "designated depository libraries *and* State Libraries." Thus, a strong case can be made that State libraries which are now included in the official lists of depository libraries and participate as such designations in the program are not legally depository libraries, although they are authorized to receive the same distribution of publications as designated depository libraries. The proposed legislation to revise Title 44 in the 96th Congress (H.R. 5424) would have corrected this situation since it includes State Libraries as one of the five "by law" special designations in section 707(d)(5). Indeed, in the initial Title 44 revision legislation introduced in the 96th Congress (H.R. 4572 and companion S. 1436) state libraries were not even listed in any category.

It may be recalled that Section 5 of the 1859 Act which established the policy of congressional designations did not list State Libraries as depository libraries. Another part of Section 5 had provided for distribution of journals and documents to "the governors of the States and territories." That part of Section 5 was not codified in section 501 of the *Revised Statutes* which pertains to depositories. Distribution to "executives of States and Territories" was provided by section 503 of the *Revised Statutes* which cites as authority the 1813 Resolution mentioned above.

To continue with the categories of materials authorized for distribution, Section 57 provided for distribution of Senate and House Journals. However, it reduced the number to "three libraries in each of the States and Territories to be designated by the Superintendent of Documents." Thus, not only was the number of copies reduced, but it was left to the Superintendent of Documents to designate which depository libraries would receive the Journals. The Journals were included in the Serial Set, but were not numbered documents or reports. Full distribution of the Journals was finally resumed by a 1938 Act discussed below.

However, several important categories of materials were added for depository distribution, which prior to 1895 included only the Journals and documents and reports of Congress. Section 73 is a lengthy 8 page list of specific titles and categories of documents. Included in the list are the following which were authorized for distribution to "depository libraries *and* to State and territorial libraries": *Revised Statutes* and *Supplement* (p. 614), *Statutes at Large* (p. 615) and *Congressional Record* (p. 618).

However, the most significant addition was in Section 58 which provided that "all publications of the Executive Departments not intended for their especial use, but made for distribution . . . shall be at once delivered to the Superintendent of Documents for distribution to designated depositories *and* State and territorial libraries." In the case of departmental publications, it should be noted that the 1895 Act set a precedent by making a distinction as to which publications shall be controlled bibliographically, and which shall be distributed to depository libraries. Some people tend to think they are the same. The "comprehensive index" required by Section 62 of the 1895 Act should include *all* Executive department publications, except those confidential in nature. Section 62 is still in effect, and is codified as Section 1710, Title 44, *U.S. Code*. However, the section on depository distribution of Executive department publications limits them to those "not intended for their especial use, but made for distribution." This limitation was further expanded and interpreted in Section 1 of the Depository Library of 1962, which was codified in Section 1902, Title 44, as follows:

Government publications, except those determined by their issuing components to be required for official use only or for strictly administrative or operational purposes which have no public interest or educational value and publications classified for reasons of national security, shall be made available to depository libraries . . . for public information.

It is of interest to note that the proposed Title 44 revision legislation in the 96th Congress (H.R. 5424) would have made identical the categories of publications subject to bibliographic control, and to depository distribution. It accepted the limited definition of "government publication" in Section 1902 (with essentially the same language) and applied it to depository libraries in Section 707(a)(1) and to the "comprehensive cumulative index" in Section 705(a)(1). There was also another significant (and subtle) difference in the definition of "government publication" in H.R. 5424 in Section 101(3) which thus applied to both depository distribution and bibliographic control in chapter 7. It deleted the provision in present Section 1902, Title 44 "except those determined by their issuing components" and thereby transferred responsibility from the issuing agency to the Superintendent of Documents (retitled Director of Distribution Services, National Publications Agency) for determining if a publication is exempt from depository distribution, and also central bibliographic control, if it is administrative or operational. Section 101(3), H.R. 5424 also deleted the words—"which have no public interest or educational value." As presently structured, the use of these terms is subject to different interpretation. A narrow interpretation is that administrative and operational publications have no public interest or educational value, and therefore all such publications are exempt. A broader interpretation is that some administrative and operational publications have public interest or educational value, and therefore all such publications are not automatically exempt but determination must be made on an individual basis. The definition of "government publication" and interpretation of exceptions authorized is important since it affects the types of publications which may be made available for distribution to depository libraries, and thus become available to the public for free access.

The 1895 Act is also important for expanding the depository library system to include other than Congressional designations, and adding the first "by law" designations. It unintentionally established State Libraries as "by law" depositories by the structure of language used in the distribution formulae: i.e., "depository libraries *and* State and territorial libraries." However, it intentionally added a second category of "by law" depositories in Section 98 which provided that "the libraries of the eight Executive Departments, of the United States Military Academy, and United States Naval Academy are hereby constituted designated depositories of Government publications." This was the beginning of the dilution of the depository library system. In his incomplete, but continuing research this author has not yet discovered the rationale for this provision.

The 1895 Act also contained two other important sections which are particularly germane to this analysis of depository libraries as a system for public access to government information. These are Section 70 pertaining to "Investigation of Depositories" and Section 74 with the side reference note, "Publications to Officials", which includes the first free public access clause.

Section 70 provides that

the Superintendent of Documents shall thoroughly investigate the condition of all libraries that are now designated depositories, and whenever he shall ascertain that the number of books in any such library, other than college libraries, is below one thousand, other than Government publications, or it has ceased to be maintained as a public library, he shall strike the same from the list.

To move the discussion ahead, this Section 70 of the 1895 Act was revised by Section 6 of the Depository Library Act of 1962. This revision was codified as Section 1909, Title 44 which reads as follows:

The designated depository libraries shall report to the Superintendent of Documents at least every two years concerning their condition. The Superintendent of Documents shall make first hand investigation of conditions for which need is indicated and include the results of investigations in his annual report. When he ascertains the number of books in a depository library is below ten thousand, other than Government publications, or it has ceased to be maintained so as to be *accessible to the public*, or that the Government publications which have been furnished the library have not been properly maintained, he shall delete the library from the list of depository libraries.

Thus, adopting a strict interpretation, the 1962 Act diluted the inspection authority of the Superintendent of Documents. The 1895 Act directed him to "thoroughly investigate" all depositories. The 1962 Act authorizes him to investigate only those depositories "for which the need is indicated." And how is the need to be indicated? Namely, by the requirement that depositories report every two years concerning their condition. What had happened after 1895 was that the Superintendent of Documents either did not ask for, or have authorized the travel funds to make the inspections required by the 1895 Act. Thus, in 1950 he inaugurated the biennial mail survey which he continues to use, and which was written into the 1962 Act in Section 6 and codified as Section 1909, Title 44. The 1962 Act also raised the minimum number of books from 1,000 to 10,000 and deleted "other than college libraries." However, more important for this consideration of public access is that the requirement of the 1895 Act that a depository shall be "maintained as a public library" was changed in 1962 to "maintained so as to be accessible to the public." If this 1895 provision had been interpreted strictly, many private college libraries would have lost their designations before 1962. However, depository librarians through the Depository Library Council to the Public Printer have influenced the Superintendent of Documents to adopt a liberal interpretation of Section 1909, Title 44. In 1975 he established a formal inspection program with three inspectors who attempt to inspect each depository at least every three years. The Council also prepared and adopted on October 18, 1977, *Guidelines for the Depository Library System*, which have been incorporated into the GPO inspection form.

Of greater importance to this discussion of public access is Section 74 of the 1895 Act which is the predecessor to the "free use" clause in present

Section 1911 of Title 44 that partisans point to as stating the basic purpose of the depository library system. Section 74 has the side reference note "Publications to officials", and the complete text is as follows:

Government publications furnished to judicial and executive officers of the United States for their official use shall not become the property of those officers, but on expiration of their official term shall be by them delivered to their successors in office and all government publications delivered to designated depositories or other libraries shall be for public use without charge.

Section 8 of the Depository Library Act of 1962 revised the language of Section 74 as follows:

All government publications of a permanent nature which are furnished by authority of law to officers (except Members of Congress) of the United States Government for their official use shall be stamped "Property of the United States Government", and shall be preserved by such officers and by them delivered to their successors in office as part of the property appertaining to the office. Government publications which are furnished to depository libraries shall be made available for the free use of the general public...

Rather than stating the basic purpose of the depository library system, the "free use"clause in Section 1911 merely states one of the conditions which depositories must observe to gain, and retain their designation. Indeed, proposed Title 44 revision in the 96th Congress continues this tradition. H.R. 5424 in Section 707(e)(1)(B) uses the term "permit free public access to such publications" as one of the two requirements which a depository library must meet. Again, nowhere in the present law, or the proposed Title 44 revision is there a strong statement as to the basic purpose of the depository library system. About the only official statement in the legislative history which states the basic purpose of the system will be found in Senate Report 87-1587 on H.R. 8141 which became the Depository Library Act of 1962. This will be discussed below.

Following the General Printing Act of 1895, the next major revision of the depository library program was the Depository Library Act of 1962 which has already been referred to extensively above. However, several significant changes were made between 1895 and 1962 which were incorporated into the 1962 Act. Section 4 of an Act of March 1, 1907 (24 *Stat.* 1014) with miscellaneous amendments to the 1895 Printing Act provided that "all land grant colleges shall be constituted as depositories for public documents subject to the provisions and limitations of depository laws." Thus, a third category of "by law" designations was created to join state libraries and federal libraries. This author is unable to find in the legislative history the justification for this action. His university library, however, obtained its depository designation in 1925 under this provision.

Joint Resolution no. 3 of January 5, 1908 (35 *Stat*. 566) relating to public printing and binding provided that departmental publications incorporated into the Serial Set as congressional documents would be furnished to depositories in the departmental edition, rather than in the Serial Set edition. Prior to 1908 depositories did not receive all volumes in the Serial Set. The main exceptions had been reports on private bills. During the 19th Century many annual reports and serial publications of the executive departments were also published as congressional documents in the Serial Set. The number of these duplicate editions was reduced considerably in the early 1900s and especially in the 1920s. A major overhaul of the Serial Set in 1979 reduced the number of such duplicate editions to four: U.S. Budget; appendix to the U.S. Budget; Economic Report of the President; and U.S. Army Corps of Engineers rivers and harbors reports.

In 1913 a lengthy 74 page sundry appropriations act approved June 23, 1913 includes a provision in Section 5 (38 *Stat*. 75) that "libraries heretofore designated by law as depositories...shall hereafter, during their existence, continue such receipt" of publications. This provision made then current and subsequent designations permanent as long as the depository fulfilled the minimum legal requirements, unless it voluntarily vacated the designation. Previously a designation was subject to removal without cause upon change of a Senator or Representative—or indeed at any time. However, there is no evidence that there was any wholesale removal of designations upon change of congressmen. This provision was incorporated into the 1962 Act and is codified in Section 1910, Title 44. The 1962 Act further provided that if following reapportionment, the number of Congressional designations exceeded the new limit, a depository would not lose its designation.

The 1923 Legislative Branch Appropriations Act approved March 20, 1922 contained a provision under funds appropriated to the Superintendent of Documents that "no part of this sum shall be used to supply depository libraries any documents, books, or other printed matter not requested by such libraries." (42 *Stat*. 436) Thus, all depositories became "selective." Previously they were required to accept all materials distributed by the Superintendent of Documents. The annual reports of the Superintendent of Documents during the 1910s contains many reports of depositories leaving boxes unopened for long periods of time, and of documents stacked on the floors, in attics, or in other inaccessible storage places. In this day of 3 or more depository boxes a day, we may find this hard to believe when back in the 1920s there might be only 3 or 4 boxes a month! A similar provision was contained in every subsequent Legislative Branch Appropriations Act until 1962. The Depository Library Act of 1962 enacted into law this provision as well as the administrative procedures which had been adopted by GPO to implement the 1922 revision. These are codified in Section 1904, Title 44 as follows: "The Superintendent of Documents shall currently issue a classified list of Government publications in suitable form, containing annotations of contents and listed by item identification numbers to facilitate the selection of only those publications needed by depository libraries."

Probably the most important amendment between 1895 and 1962 was Public Law 75-70, approved June 25, 1938. (52 *Stat.* 1206) which significantly increases the categories of materials distributed to depository libraries. This Act provided that the Public Printer shall furnish to depositories

the Journals of the Senate and House of Representatives, all publications not confidential in character, printed upon requisition of any Congressional committee, all Senate and House public bills and resolutions, and all reports on private bills and concurrent or simple resolutions.

If a library has a comprehensive hard copy collection of government documents, the librarians there may have notices that many hearings published before 1940 are not held. The reason is that Committee hearings were not added to depository distribution until 1939. The Act also authorized distribution of committee prints, but not many were distributed until about five years ago since committees often claimed their prints were "administrative" publications and thus exempt from depository distribution. The Act also added bills and resolutions to the new categories not distributed before. Also added were reports on private bills, which as mentioned above were not included with the Serial Set volumes sent to depository libraries. It also resumed full depository distribution of Congressional Journals, which since 1895 had been limited to 3 sets per state.

The 1938 Act is, of course, very important from a public access point of view since it increased significantly the categories of congressional materials conveniently available for public access in depository libraries. However, it is important for another reason in developing the theme of this article. The legislation was initiated by librarians, and not by the Superintendent of Documents who is responsible for operation of the program— or by any element of the Federal Government concerned with improving free access to government information. The legislation was pushed by the ALA Public Documents Committee, which was concerned about the limited amount of materials distributed to depositories. Indeed, the Public Documents Committee wanted to include in the legislative package so called "non-GPO" materials. The Committee had become aware during the 1930s that with the expansion of the federal government under President Franklin D. Roosevelt's "New Deal" an increasing number of government publications were not printed by the Government Printing Office, but by agencies in-house using "processed" or other near print methods of reproduction. The departmental publications in the depository program had become limited to those printed by the GPO; this practice was continued until 1962. Even today despite the marked increase during the past five years of the number of "non-GPO" publications added to the program (primarily in microfiche) the bulk of the depository publications are those printed by or under contract to the GPO Central Printing Plant in Washington. It has been only in the last five years that GPO has also made an effort to incorporate into depository distribution those publications printed under contract to GPO Regional Procurement Offices.

This author's thesis is that the depository library program is basically a library sponsored and initiated program for the benefit of libraries, and not a program of overriding concern to the federal government or to the general public. The "free use" clause in Section 1911 does not state the basic purpose of the program—that the Government designed and uses the program as its main vehicle to provide the public free access to government information. Rather, the legislative history clearly shows that the "free use" clause is just one of several conditions which participating libraries must observe to obtain government publications free and to retain their designation.

Library community interest—and relative disinterest by the Government—are obviously apparent in the passage of the Depository Library Act of 1962, and in the recent attempt to revise Title 44 and increase the types of informational materials to be made available. Indeed, such a situation was present during the early history of the depository library program as indicated in a 1980 doctoral dissertation by Sarah Jordan Miller at Columbia University: *The Depository Library System: a History of the Distribution of Federal Government Publications to Libraries of the United States from the Early Years of the Nation to 1895*. Her main theme can be found in the abstract published in *Dissertation Abstracts International* vol. 41, no. 4, October 1980 (p. 1264A). She concludes that the basic depository legislation of 1857-59 described above was precipitated by a resolution adopted at the 1853 Librarians Conference. As for the 1895 Printing Act, Miller concludes that its "provisions . . . paralleled closely the recommendations which had emanated from the library community in the preceding years, and the program which the Act began was one which the library community has largely formulated."

The Depository Library Act of 1962 had its origins in investigations in 1956 during the 84th Congress by the Subcommittee to Study Federal Printing and Paperwork of the Committee on House Administration that found problems in the depository library program. Legislation designed to reform the program and consolidate existing law was introduced in the 85th Congress as H.R. 9186, amended as H.R. 11042 and passed by the

House in 1958 as H.R. 13140. However, the Senate did not act on the bill, either in the 85th Congress, or during the 86th Congress when it was reintroduced and passed the House again as H.R. 519. During the 87th Congress the bill was reintroduced as H.R. 8141 and again passed the House. The Senate then considered the bill, held hearings, and reported an amended bill which passed in 1962.

The Depository Library Act of 1962 incorporated and consolidated many early provisions of law. However, it made four important revisions in the program: (1) increased the number of designations authorized each Representative and each Senator from one to two; (2) increased the number of federal libraries authorized from the Cabinet Departments and military academy libraries in order to provide additional depositories to independent agencies, and to each major bureau, office or division within executive departments and independent agencies; (3) expanded the categories of depository materials by authorizing the distribution of "non-GPO" publications; and (4) authorized two regional libraries in each state that could permit the selective depositories to discard materials after holding them five years.

One of the major problems and complaints of depository libraries was that they were required to retain permanently depository materials. During the 1950s the Superintendent of Documents had authorized the establishment of experimental regional libraries in Wisconsin and New York that could permit selective depositories in those states to discard materials after 25 years. The 1962 Act reduced the mandatory retention period to 5 years, and required regional depositories to accept all materials, hold them permanently (with limited exceptions) and to provide reference, interlibrary loan, and assistance to selective depositories in the disposal of unwanted materials. These provisions are codified in Section 1912, Title 44.

As mentioned earlier, the library community had attempted in 1938 to have "non-GPO" publications included in depository distribution. This provision as proposed in the 1962 bill was opposed by executive and independent agencies, and given only lukewarm support by the Superintendent of Documents. (This was after all a librarian initiated bill, not a government agency bill.) There was another provision in the 1962 bill which was vigorously opposed by the Superintendent of Documents: i.e., to provide microform copies of older materials to regional depositories in order to reduce their requirements for space. The library community did not press this provision, and appeared pleased to compromise after gaining the non-GPO provision. However, after the bill passed, implementation of the non-GPO provision was grudging and slow. Congress refused to provide funds in 1963 for the new program, and the following year, only a small amount was given to start a pilot project with

Census Bureau publications. During the 1960s only a few other agencies were added to the program. Finally, the program got off the ground in the mid-1970s after GPO made a 180 degree turn and started its own microform program. JCP had also added Section 41-2 to the *Government Printing and Binding Regulations* with the 24th edition, April 1977, and required agencies to furnish GPO with two copies only of such non-GPO publications: one copy for cataloging and bibliographic control in the *Monthly Catalog*; and the other copy to prepare a microform master from which additional microfiche could be manufactured for depository distribution. One feature of the 1962 non-GPO provision which resulted in noncompliance, or only grudging compliance was that the issuing agencies are required to pay from their own appropriations for the added copies furnished GPO for depository distribution. With respect to the "free use" clause, the history of the non-GPO provision illustrates that this is a library oriented program, and the Government does not yet see it as a primary vehicle for providing information to the general public.

This was further illustrated in the provision which expanded the number of federal libraries which could obtain designations. The hearings indicated that the provision was enacted to provide government libraries with a convenient centralized method for automatic distribution of publications of other agencies for use by their own personnel. There is no indication it was enacted primarily to provide free access for the public. However, the number of additional federal libraries requesting a designation has fortunately been low; as of April 1979 only 65 out of an estimated 2000 plus federal libraries that might qualify. This expanded provision of "by law" designations for more federal libraries is codified in section 1907, Title 44.

However, the main purpose of the Depository Library Act of 1962 was to increase the number of non-federal depositories. While it was found that more designations were wanted and needed; it was also found that there was mal-distribution in the designations. In 1962 there were 120 vacancies, of which 116 were Congressional designations. Out of a maximum possible number of 720 designations, 594 had been filled. This casts doubt on the argument that the basic purpose of the system is to provide free public access throughout the country within the 435 congressional districts.

In 1972 this author prepared a tenth anniversary review of the enactment of the Depository Library Act of 1962 with emphasis on implementation of the provision for regional libraries. He found that the situation was again approaching the critical and paradoxial stage it had ten years earlier. There were again a number of libraries that wished to, and deserved to acquire depository status, but were unable to due to lack of congressional vacancies in their district or state. Meanwhile, there was again a large number of congressional vacancies (195 of which 22 were Senatorial and 173 were Representatives), for which there were no volunteer libraries. Again in 1972 the same solution was proposed as had been a decade earlier; i.e., identical bills sponsored by 48 representatives were introduced to increase the number of representative designations from 2 to 3 each. None of the bills passed. In the review, this author also found that the depository library program is dominated by the academic library. Of 1080 depositories in 1972, 711 (or 65.8%) were academic libraries; 249 (or 23%) were public libraries; 65 (or 5.8%) were state libraries; 9 (or 1.8%) were special libraries; and 27 (or 5.3%) were federal libraries.[3]

Of the 711 academic libraries, 27 were law school libraries, and 29 were 2 year community or junior college libraries. The following percentages apply to the 509 new depositories designated between 1962 and 1972: 358 (or 70.3%) were academic libraries; 108 (or 21.2%) were public libraries; 9 (or 1.8%) were state libraries; 7 (or 1.4%) were special libraries; and 27 (or 5.3%) were federal libraries.

This author has now made a similar analysis of depository status as of April 1979 (see Tables 2-1 and 2-2) which is the effective date of the last complete list available. The 1979 JCP Committee Print was expanded to provide a listing of depositories in the traditional arrangement by congressional district, plus an additional second listing arranged alphabetically by city similar to the familiar listing in the September issue of the *Monthly Catalog*. Incidentally, the *Monthly Catalog's* September list was discontinued in 1979 and did not appear in 1980. The GPO has promised to renew the listing. Meanwhile, the JCP list did not appear in 1980 either.*

In 1979 there were 143 vacancies of which 126 were Representative and 17 Senatorial. However, this number could have been higher, since 35 accredited law school libraries had not vacated their congressional designations. Seven highest state appellate courts had used a state library designation forcing the state library to use a congressional designation. Thirteen districts had no depositories; and 49 congressional districts had only one depository.

Academic libraries still accounted for nearly two-thirds of all depositories with 885 (or 65.4%) including law school libraries. There were 112 law school libraries (8.6%). Of these 71 were located on the same campus or city as the main university library, also a depository. Two university campuses had three designations. There were 69 land grant college designations (5.3%), 674 other college and university libraries, and 37 two year community or junior college libraries.

*Editor's Note: The JCP list appeared in 1981, but after the conclusion of the conference and the preparation of the proceedings.

Public libraries lost ground—down from 23% in 1972 to 21.2% in 1979 with 277 libraries. There were 55 state libraries (4.2%) and 34 highest state appellate court libraries (2.6%). The percentage of federal libraries decreased slightly. Of the 65 federal libraries, 10 were Executive Department libraries, 5 were military academy libraries, 22 were libraries of subordinate bureaus, offices, etc. of executive agencies (many of them military schools), 11 were judicial branch (most of the circuit court libraries, plus the Supreme Court), and 3 were legislative branch libraries (GAO and 2 at LC). There were 21 special libraries (1.6%); 8 of these were county or city law libraries, and 2 were municipal reference libraries. Some of the 11 other special libraries may have fitted into other categories, but it was difficult to identify the type of library by the title.

However, further analysis of these figures is needed. For example, what is the size and location of depositories with respect to population densities? What are the characteristics of the districts which do not have any, or only one, depository: are they in densely populated metropolitan districts with depositories located at short distances in neighboring districts, or are they in sparsely populated districts with large land areas requiring extensive travel between population centers? If they are academic libraries, are the institutions public or private? In this regard, the October 1979 issue of *Information World*, a spokesman for the information industry reported the results of an informal survey on how "free" was access to selected depositories in metropolitan areas. It found that some libraries with depository designations were closed to the public, particularly, as might be expected, the private institution libraries; and admittance was limited to staff, faculty and students. Special provision had to be made to allow access to the general public. Members of the general public seeking access would have to know first of all that the library was a depository, and secondly that one of the conditions of obtaining depository material was free access by the public to its depository collection, but not to the entire library.

Between 1962 and 1979 (when major Title 44 revision legislation was introduced in the 96th Congress), two amendments were made to the depository library program; these added two more categories of "by law" designations. Public Law 92-368 approved August 10, 1972 (86 *Stat.* 507) authorized the Public Printer to designate as depositories upon request "the highest appellate court of a State." This law was codified as added Section 1915, Title 44. The bill passed both houses without hearings being held. It set a bad precedent by exempting such libraries from section 1911 with its "free use" clause and the provisions to dispose of unwanted materials after five years when approved by a regional depository. What purpose should such depositories serve? The reports from both house (H. Rept. 92-1201 and S. Rept. 92-255) do not give a clue.

Table 2-1: Number of Depository Libraries (As of April 1979) by Type and/or Designation of Library

	1	2	3	4	5	6	7	8	9	10	11	12	13	14	15	16
	College/University			Law School		Acad. Libs	Publ Libs	State Libs		State	Ct.L	Federal Libraries			Spec. Libs	Libs
	4yr+ coll.	2yr. coll.	Land Gmt	cong. des.	by law	Total	Total	state Lib	cong. des.	stateL	Ct.	Exec/ MilAc	SubEx/ IndA	Jndi/ Leg.	City LawL	Total
Alabama	11	3	2	1	–	17	3	–	1	1	1	–/–	1/–	–/–	–	–
Alasaka	1	1	1	1	–	3	1	1	–	–	1	–/–	–/–	–/–	–	–
Arizona	6	–	1	1	1	8	3	1	–	–	1	–/–	–/–	–/–	–	–
Arkansas	11	2	2	–	1	14	1	1	+	–	1	–/–	2/–	1/–	–	–
California	36	1	1	5	8	51	43	1	–	–	1	–/–	–/1	1/–	4	5
Canal Zone	–	–	–	–	–	–	–	–	–	–	–	–/–	–/–	–/–	–	–
Colorado	10	1	1	–	1	13	5	1	–	–	1	–/1	1/–	1/–	–	–
Connecticut	9	1	1	–	1	12	5	1	1	1	–	–/1	–/–	–/–	1	1
Delaware	–	1	2	1	–	4	1	1	1	1	–	–/–	–/–	–/–	1	1
Dist. of Columbia	1	–	1	–	3	5	1	–	–	–	1	9/–	8/11	2/3	–	–
Florida	16	3	1	2	2	24	11	1	–	–	–	–/–	–/–	–/–	–	–
Georgia	15	2	1	1	2	21	4	1	–	–	–	–/–	–/–	–/–	–	–
Guam	–	–	1	–	–	1	1	–	–	–	–	–/–	–/–	–/–	–	–
Hawaii	2	1	1	–	1	5	2	1	–	–	1	–/–	–/–	–/–	2	2
Idaho	5	–	1	–	1	7	1	1	–	–	–	–/–	–/–	–/–	–	–
Illinois	29	3	1	2	6	41	11	1	–	–	1	–/–	–/–	1/–	1	1
Indiana	20	–	1	–	3	24	7	1	–	–	–	–/–	–/–	–/–	–	–
Iowa	9	2	1	1	1	14	5	1	–	–	1	–/–	–/–	–/–	–	–
Kansas	8	1	1	2	1	12	2	1	1	–	–	–/–	–/–	–/–	–	–
Kentucky	10	1	2	2	3	15	2	1	1	1	1	–/–	–/–	–/–	–	–
Louisiana	15	–	2	1	2	20	2	–	–	–	1	–/–	–/–	1/–	–	–
Maine	6	–	1	–	1	8	2	1	–	–	1	–/–	–/–	–/–	–	–
Maryland	9	2	1	–	1	13	2	1	–	–	1	1/1	2/–	–/–	–	–
Massachusetts	15	–	2	–	3	20	8	1	–	–	1	–/–	–/–	1/–	1	3
Michigan	23	–	1	1	4	29	15	1	1	1	1	–/–	–/1	–/–	1	1
Minnesota	11	–	1	–	3	15	7	–	1	1	–	–/–	–/–	1/–	–	–
Mississippi	6	–	2	2	–	10	–	1	1	1	1	–/–	–/1	1/–	–	–
Missouri	16	–	3	1	3	23	4	1	1	–	1	–/–	–/–	1/–	–	–
Montana	4	–	1	–	–	5	–	1	1	–	–	–/–	–/–	–/–	–	–
Nebraska	7	–	1	–	–	8	2	1	1	–	–	–/–	–/–	–/–	–	–

	1	2	3	4	5	6	7	8	9	10	11	12	13	14	15	16
Nevada	2	-	1	-	-	3	1	1	-	-	-	1	-/-	-/-	-	-
New Hampshire	4	-	1	-	-	5	2	1	1	-	-	-	-/-	-/-	-	1
New Jersey	18	-	1	2	-	21	19	1	1	1	-	-	-/-	-/-	1	1
New Mexico	5	1	1	1	-	8	0	-	1	-	1	-	-/-	-/-	-	-
New York	49	2	2	6	2	60	18	1	1	1	-	1	-/2	1/-	-	3
North Carolina	24	-	2	2	-	28	4	1	1	-	-	1	-/-	-/-	-	-
North Dakota	4	-	1	-	-	5	2	1	-	2	-	1	-/-	-/-	-	1
Ohio	33	1	1	4	-	39	13	1	2	-	-	1	-/-	1/-	-	1
Oklahoma	11	-	-	2	2	15	4	1	-	-	-	1	-/-	1/-	-	-
Oregon	10	-	-	1	1	12	1	1	-	-	-	1	-/-	1/-	1	-
Pennsylvania	31	3	2	3	1	40	15	1	1	-	-	-	-/-	1/-	1	1
Puerto Rico	2	-	1	1	-	4	-	-	-	-	-	-	-/-	-/-	-	-
Rhode Island	3	-	1	-	-	4	4	1	-	-	-	-	-/-	1/-	-	-
South Carolina	11	-	2	-	-	13	4	1	1	-	-	1	-/-	-/-	-	-
South Dakota	6	-	1	-	-	7	2	1	1	-	-	1	-/-	-/-	-	-
Tennessee	12	2	2	2	-	18	4	1	1	1	-	1	-/-	-/1	-	-
Texas	41	3	1	2	1	48	10	1	1	1	-	1	-/-	-/-	-	-
Utah	6	-	1	2	-	9	-	1	-	-	-	-	-/-	-/-	-	-
Vermont	5	-	1	1	-	7	7	1	1	-	-	-	-/-	-/-	-	-
Virginia	16	2	2	2	1	23	4	1	1	-	1	1	-/-	4/-	1/-	-
Virgin Islands	-	-	1	-	-	1	2	-	-	-	-	-	-/-	-/-	-	-
Washington	7	1	1	1	1	11	6	1	1	-	-	1	-/-	-/-	-	-
West Virginia	9	-	2	-	-	11	2	1	1	-	-	1	-/-	-/-	-	-
Wisconsin	14	1	1	-	-	15	8	-	-	1	-	1	1/-	-/-	1	1
Wyoming	3	-	1	-	-	6	1	1	1	1	1	1	-/-	-/-	1	1
	637	37	69	35	77	855	277	41	55	14	8	26	10/5	22/14	11/3	8	21
	51.6%		5.3%	8.6%		65.4%	21.2%		4.2%			2.6%		5/0%			1.6%

COLUMN NOTES:
1. 4 years or more college or university.
2. 2 year community or junior college
3. land grant university designation
4. designated by a Senator or Representative
5. special designation for accredited law school library under P.L. 95-261
6. total for academic libraries including law schools
7. total for public libraries
8. State Library using by law designation
9. State Library designated by Senator or Representative
10. Highest state appellate court using State Library desn.
11. Highest court using special designation under P.L. 92-368
12. Executive Department Libraries/Military academies
13. Subordinate bureaus, etc of exec. agencies/Independent agencies
14. Judicial branch libraries/Legislative branch libraries
15. County and/or city law libraries
16. Total for Special Libraries

Table 2-2: Number of Depository Libraries (As of April 1979) by Number of Depositories in a District

Districts in State/Territory with Number of Depositories											Dep. Total	Vacancies		
	0	1	2	3	4	5	6	7	8	9	10		Rep.	Sen.	Tot.

State/Territory	0	1	2	3	4	5	6	7	8	9	10	Dep. Total	Rep.	Sen.	Tot.
Alabama	–	1	1	2	2	–	1	–	–	–	–	23	1	–	1
Alaska	–	–	–	–	–	–	1	–	–	–	–	6	–	3	3
Arizona	–	–	2	1	–	1	1	–	–	–	–	12	2	–	2
Arkansas	–	–	–	1	2	1	1	–	–	–	–	17	1	–	1
California	–	8	20	9	3	2	–	1	–	–	–	104	12	–	12
Canal Zone	–	1	–	–	–	–	–	–	–	–	–	1	1	–	1
Colorado	–	–	–	3	1	1	1	–	–	1	–	23	1	–	1
Connecticut	–	–	2	2	1	1	1	–	–	–	–	20	–	1	1
Delaware	–	–	–	–	–	–	–	–	1	–	–	8	1	–	1
Dist. of Columbia	–	–	1	–	–	–	–	–	1	–	–	39	1	–	1
Florida	–	3	6	5	–	1	–	1	–	–	–	37	4	–	4
Georgia	–	1	4	4	–	1	–	–	–	–	–	26	2	–	2
Guam	–	–	1	–	–	–	–	–	–	–	–	2	1	–	1
Hawaii	–	–	–	–	–	1	1	–	–	–	–	11	1	–	1
Idaho	–	–	–	1	–	1	1	1	–	–	–	10	1	1	2
Illinois	2	6	7	5	2	1	–	1	–	–	–	55	10	–	10
Indiana	–	1	3	3	3	1	–	–	–	–	–	33	2	–	2
Iowa	–	–	2	–	4	–	–	–	–	–	–	20	–	1	1
Kansas	–	–	2	1	1	–	1	–	–	–	–	17	1	–	1
Kentucky	–	1	4	1	–	1	1	1	–	–	–	19	2	–	2
Louisiana	2	2	1	3	–	1	–	1	–	–	–	25	3	1	4
Maine	–	–	–	1	–	–	1	1	–	–	–	12	–	–	–
Maryland	–	1	4	1	2	–	–	–	–	–	–	20	8	–	8
Massachusetts	–	3	3	2	3	–	–	–	–	–	–	34	5	–	5
Michigan	–	2	9	2	4	–	–	–	–	–	–	48	4	–	4
Minnesota	1	1	1	3	1	–	1	–	–	–	–	24	4	–	2
Mississippi	1	1	1	1	–	–	1	–	–	–	–	12	4	2	6
Missouri	–	1	3	3	2	–	1	–	–	–	–	30	3	–	3

State															
Montana	–	1	–	–	–	–	–	1	–	–	–	8	1	2	3
Nebraska	–	–	–	1	–	–	1	–	–	–	–	12	–	–	–
Nevada	–	–	–	1	–	–	1	1	–	–	–	7	–	2	2
New Hampshire	–	–	–	–	1	–	–	–	–	–	–	9	–	1	1
New Jersey	–	2	3	7	3	1	–	–	–	–	–	41	2	–	2
New Mexico	–	–	–	–	1	–	–	–	–	–	–	10	–	–	–
New York	3	9	14	5	3	3	1	1	–	–	–	85	18	–	18
North Carolina	–	–	5	3	2	–	1	1	–	–	1	34	–	–	–
North Dakota	–	–	–	–	–	–	–	–	–	–	–	10	–	–	–
Ohio	3	–	11	7	3	–	–	1	–	–	–	55	9	–	9
Oklahoma	–	–	1	3	1	–	–	1	–	–	–	21	3	–	3
Oregon	–	–	4	–	–	1	1	–	–	–	–	16	3	–	3
Pennsylvania	1	–	16	6	1	1	–	1	–	–	–	59	4	–	4
Puerto Rico	–	–	–	–	1	–	–	–	–	–	–	4	–	–	–
Rhode Island	–	–	–	1	–	–	–	–	–	–	–	10	1	–	1
South Carolina	–	1	–	4	1	1	–	1	–	–	–	18	1	–	1
South Dakota	–	–	–	–	–	–	–	–	–	–	–	11	–	–	–
Tennessee	–	–	3	4	2	–	1	1	–	1	–	25	–	–	–
Texas	1	1	12	7	2	1	1	1	–	–	–	60	3	–	3
Utah	–	–	–	–	–	–	–	–	1	1	–	11	–	–	–
Vermont	–	–	–	–	–	–	–	–	–	–	–	8	–	–	–
Virginia	–	–	3	4	–	2	1	1	–	–	–	34	4	–	4
Virgin Islands	–	–	–	1	–	–	–	–	–	–	–	3	–	1	–
Washington	1	–	2	3	–	–	1	1	–	–	–	18	4	1	5
West Virginia	–	2	2	3	3	1	1	1	–	–	–	15	1	–	1
Wisconsin	–	–	2	1	–	1	–	–	–	–	–	26	2	1	3
Wyoming	–	–	–	–	–	–	–	–	–	1	–	9	–	1	1
	13	49	153	111	52	22	21	12	2	2	1	1307	126	17	143

Public Law 95-261 (92 *Stat.* 199) approved on April 17, 1978, but not effective until October 1, 1978 (start of FY 1979), authorized the Public Printer to designate as depository libraries upon request any accredited law school. This was codified as added Section 1916, Title 44. Bills had been introduced starting in the 92 Congress to provide special "by law" designations to law school libraries. Several of the bills introduced in the 95th Congress would have exempted them from the "free use" provision of Section 1911. However, ALA representatives insisted that such libraries must be subject to the same requirements as other depositories. The Act does exempt law school libraries from much of Section 1909, Title 44 relating to the location of new depositories: i.e. "within an area not already adequately serviced by existing depository libraries."

Title 44 revision bills in the 96th Congress proposed significant changes to the depository library program, particularly in expanding the formats of materials available for depository distribution to include machine readable data-files and audiovisual materials. They also expanded the term "government publication" to include all documents "reproduced...for official use of a Government entity" which could include any material produced at government expense such as contract reports. They also proposed that the Superintendent of Documents should maintain a complete collection of Government publications and should provide support services (including financial support) to depository libraries. The original bill introduced (H.R. 4572) also had a provision for an additional 100 depository libraries at large to be designated by the Superintendent of Documents. This provision was eliminated in H.R. 5424, which was the final amended bill introduced in the 96th Congress.

These major changes had their genesis in recommendations of the Report of the ALA Ad Hoc Committee on the Depository Library System which was approved in principle by the ALA Council on July 11, 1974 at the Annual Conference in New York City. The Committee had recommended that

'publications' shall be defined as all print and non-print documents produced at the expense of the federal government, regardless of format, method of reproduction, or source. These documents shall include, but not be limited to printed documents, slides, films, machine-readable data files, recordings, maps, audio tapes and video tapes." The Committee had also recommended that the depository library system should be "expanded into a comprehensive network of local and regional depositories, with a national depository agency at the head of the system" and that a "comprehensive and historical collection of federal publications should be maintained by the national depository agency.

The Committee recommended that regional depositories should be provided federal funds on a formula basis, and the National Depository

Agency should be authorized to designate additional depositories on a basis of need only.

However, it was these very provisions which were instrumental in the defeat of the bill. Both the Committee on Rules and Committee on Government Operations claimed jurisdiction in the bill. The Government Operations Committee effectively killed the bill when it reported out a substitute bill, "The Federal Publications Act" (H. Rept. 96-836, pt. 3) "without recommendation." This substitute bill deleted provisions for depository distribution of machine-readable data files and audiovisual materials, financial support of depositories, and creation of a comprehensive collection. Minority views in the Report by the Committee on House Administration (H. Report. 96-836, part 1) hit upon the reason for Government Operations' scuttling the bill. It quotes from one of the members of the JCP Ad Hoc Advisory Committee on Revision of Title 44 (evidently an OMB representative) that the Committee's report, and the bill, "goes beyond the scope of Title 44...and attempts to formulate an overall Federal information policy." The Committee on Government Operations has jurisdiction over information policy, and its turf had been invaded.

The Committee on Government Operations had sponsored the Paperwork Reduction Act of 1980 (H.R. 6410) approved December 11, 1980 as P.L. 96-511. Although it deals mainly with records management and the collection of information, it also has significant provisions dealing with the distribution of information, including publications. Apparently the Committee on House Administration did not claim jurisdiction or request sequential referral of the bill. Library representatives were also not asked to testify.

The Committee on Government Operations had also sponsored the Federal Information Centers Act of 1978 to authorize the permanent establishment of a system of federal information centers. (P.L. 95-491, approved October 20, 1978) The centers were begun in 1966 on a pilot basis by executive order, but had been funded annually by Congress. Some of their functions apparently duplicate some of those of depositories. Yet, there was little interest until recently by the library community in the centers, which are a strictly government operation and program. Again, the Committee on House Administration was apparently not consulted on the legislation, and in turn did not claim jurisdiction or request sequential referral. Library representatives were also not invited to testify at hearings.

On July 25, 1978 the Office of Management and Budget published in the *Federal Register* for comment a proposed policy on the dissemination of scientific and technical information. It received a number of comments from the library community that the policy failed to mention depository libraries or the requirements of Title 44 for bibliographic control. However, the proposal was intended primarily as an implementation of the responsibilities of the National Technical Information Service (NTIS) as spelled out in its charter, PL 81-776 approved September 1950, and codified as Sections 1151-1157, Title 15. The conflict was not caused by OMB but by the fact a vacuum in the area of non-GPO publications, especially technical report literature, had been created which was filled by NTIS and its predecessors, and which years later proponents of Title 44, the depository library program and the *Monthly Catalog* now belatedly claimed interest and some responsibility. A revised and expanded version of the proposal, retitled "Improved Management and Dissemination of Federal Information" was published for comment in the *Federal Register* on June 9, 1980. It mentioned depository libraries, JCP, GPO, and the requirements of Title 44. However, implementation of the policy has been delayed by the change in Administrations. The proposed policy is also subject to further change with the implementation of the Paperwork Reduction Act of 1980 that established an Office of Information and Regulatory Affairs in OMB. Under the Carter Administration there was a close alliance between the staffs of the Committee on Government Operations and OMB. We must wait to see if this alliance and close working relationship continues under the Reagan administration and the new OMB Director, David Stockman who was formerly a member of the Committee on House Administration as a Representative from Michigan in the 96th Congress.

We must also wait to see what effect the change in control, not only of the Administration, but also of the Senate will have on the Joint Committee on Printing. One of the first acts passed by the 97th Congress was a bill introduced by the Republican controlled Senate Committee on Rules and Administration (S. 272) to increase the membership of the JCP from six to ten members. The bill passed the Senate on February 3, and the House on February 5. It is the Senate's turn to chair the Committee, and it was expected that Sen. Charles Mathias (R.-Md.), Chairman of the Senate Committee on Rules and Administration would be elected as JCP chairman. It was also expected that Mathias would reduce the number of JCP staff members by not filling two vacancies. In the 96th Congress, the Senate Committee was lukewarm on proposed Title 44 revision. In the House, H.R. 5424 was strongly opposed by the minority members of all three committees that considered the bills (House Administration, Government Operations, and Rules) all of whom joined in submitting very critical minority views in all three parts of House Report 96-836.

This again illustrated that the depository program is not viewed as a major government program to provide free access to government information, when the executive department agency responsible for the development of a national information policy showed ignorance of the depository library program. However, following this incident and the recent White House Conference on Libraries and Information Services the executive branch is becoming aware of the existence of the program. Another factor which has many advantages, but in the case of above and similar cases, may be a disadvantage is that the program is operated by and supervised by the legislative branch as represented by the Government Printing Office and Joint Committee on Printing. Executive agencies claim that control over their printing by legislative branch agencies is in violation of the constitutional provisions of separation of powers. JCP also gets its membership from the Committee on House Administration and Senate Committee on Rules and Administration. These are not considered to be major congressional committees and assignments are not highly prized or sought after.

In tracing the law and reports on the bills this author finds only one statement in the long legislative history which describes and states the purpose of the depository library program. It can be found in Senate Report 87-1587 on H.R. 8141, the Depository Library Act of 1962.

The depository library system is a long established cooperative program between the Federal Government and designated major libraries throughout the United States under which certain classes of Government publications are supplied free of cost to those libraries for the purpose of making such publications more readily accessible to the American public. (p.3)

This statement highlights a significant and key feature about the program. It is a cooperative program between the Federal Government and the library community. In a cooperative program each side expects to gain equal or greater benefits in comparison to the obligations or expenses which it bears.

The library community gets a wide selection of government publications free of charge. It gets them conveniently on automatic distribution and with preassigned standard classification numbers which simply processing and shelving. These publications are primarily those needed to meet the needs of the library's own patrons and clientele. In accepting the publications, a depository accepts a minimum number of not too onerous obligations to make them available free of charge to any member of the general public that may also wish to use them. A depository, of course, also incurs a considerable amount of expense in providing staff and facilities to process, maintain, and provide reference service on the collection. On the other hand, the Federal Government pays the costs of printing and distributing these publications which according to recent GPO figures amounts to approximately $12,000 for each depository library in a system of over 1300 libraries. As for benefits, the Government apparently subscribes to the philosophy that it has a responsibility in a democratic society to keep its citizens informed of its activities, and it finds that using a network of existing libraries is an economical way of accomplishing this basic mission rather than starting its own network of libraries or information centers.

In making a case for federal financial support to depositories, librarians argue that depositories pay more into the program than the Federal government. Recent figures have been advanced that it costs $325,000 annually to maintain a regional collection, and that it costs $10 per item to process and service a depository document.[4] This argument ignores the very basic cooperative feature of the program, and also that it is really a library initiated program. Libraries gain their designations through requests, which they voluntarily submit. They are not ordered by their Representative or Senator to assume a designation. They may voluntarily give up their designation at any time. The fact of the matter is that designations are highly prized and eagerly sought after by less fortunate libraries that are unable to obtain them. The selective depositories which constitute the vast majority may select only those items which they want to receive. They are not forced to take any item which may have little interest to the library's regular clientele or which the Government thinks should be accessible to the general public in the congressional district which the library serves. The Depository Library Council has recommended that depositories should select a minimum of 25% of the available items. It has also drawn up a list of 23 titles which it believes every depository should accept including the *Code of Federal Regulations* and *U.S. Code.* However, this is not (and can not be) mandatory. If a library did not have depository status (or before it obtained its designation) it would still want to get many of the publications anyway which it selects. If it were not a depository it would be forced to pay the GPO inflated sales prices with their 300 percent plus markup. It would soon learn that a large percent of depository publications are not sold by GPO, and it would spend a considerable amount of time and money in obtaining these publications (if it were able to) from issuing agencies. In addition to the cost of the publications themselves, the library would have much higher costs for acquisition and processing, and it would still have the same maintenance and service costs which it would have as a depository.

The depository library program is a library initiated program. Major changes in the program have been initiated by the library community to meet its particular requirements for the benefit of its clientele, although the public has indirectly benefitted. Libraries initiated changes to provide for the selective feature in 1922 and to establish regional depositories in 1962 in order to get a system for early discarding of unwanted materials. The general public has benefitted most by those initiatives of the library community that have resulted in expanding the categories and types of materials distributed to depositories. Libraries were instrumental in having departmental publications added in 1895; of adding Congressional hearings and committee prints in 1938; of adding non-GPO publications in 1962, and then monitoring the program to insist that GPO take a more active role to gain compliance with the program by executive branch agencies.

In conclusion, this article has traced the historical development of the depository library program, and has analyzed some significant features of the program including its strengths and weaknesses. It has not made recommendations for improvement since the article by Charles R. McClure analyzes the structure of the current program and makes recommendations for a restructured depository library program.

References

1. Bernadine E. Hoduski, "The Federal Depository Library System: What Is Its Basic Job?", *Drexel Library Quarterly*, 10, (January-April 1974): 108.

2. LeRoy C. Schwarzkopf, "The Depository Library Program and Access by the Public to Official Publications of the United States Government", *Government Publications Review*, 5 (1978): 154

3. LeRoy C. Schwarzkopf, *Regional Libraries and the Depository Library Act of 1962*, pp. 1-6 (available from ERIC Documents Reproduction Service as ED 066 177)

4. U.S. Congress. Joint Committee on Printing. *Federal Government Printing and Publishing: Policy Issues; Report of the Ad Hoc Advisory Committee on Revision of Title 44*, Committee Print, 1979, p. 45.

STRUCTURAL ANALYSIS OF THE DEPOSITORY SYSTEM: A PRELIMINARY ASSESSMENT

By Charles R. McClure

During the late 1970s and early 1980s considerable discussion took place regarding the method by which the United States Government should distribute government publications to the citizens of the country. The principal means the Government Printing Office (GPO) has employed to accomplish its statuatory responsibilities has been the operation of a depository library system. For more than half a century, the depository library system has been promoted as the most important means by the Government to distribute materials and encourage their availability to the general population. However, few formal attempts have been made to analyze critically the structure of that system, and how it affects the overall effectiveness of the depository system.

The purpose of this chapter is to examine the depository library system in terms of its structure, identify factors that impact on the structural arrangement of the system, identify critical assumptions that must be recognized and considered when analyzing the depository system's structure, and make recommendations that may assist in the re-design of the system. General systems concepts will be used to address these issues. The thesis of this chapter is that there has been inadequate research investigating the effectiveness of the depository structure. Further, the library/information community must encourage the formal evaluative review of the system, based on clear measures of performance and effectiveness *before* any meaningful changes can be suggested to improve the existing system.

Much has been written regarding the depository library system during recent years, and the following sources can provide useful background information as to the history and current status of the depository library system: Morehead,[1] Buckley,[2] Schwarzkopf,[3] and *Instructions To Depository Libraries.*[4] No attempt will be made here to review or critically assess the various writings regarding the depository library system. In general, these writings have not reported empirical data related to the effectiveness of the system nor have they suggested methods by which formal evaluation of the system could be accomplished. Although this chapter will not present empirical data as a basis to analyze the system, it will pursue a deductive approach that can set a framework by which factors can be identified to develop a formal evaluative review of the depository structure.[5]

The comments and suggestions that will be made here are intended to improve a depository library system that provides adequate document delivery, bibliographic control, and publicity for selected government publications. Further, compared to most other countries, the United States depository library system is better organized to distribute government information. One should not lose sight of this fact as the chapter presents a framework for a preliminary assessment of the system. Although the emphasis is on the structure (the organizational arrangement and relationship among system components) of the system, the functional aspects (the purpose or activities of the system and its components) of the system that affect the structure cannot be ignored. Thus, the emphasis will be placed on the depository structure but when necessary, functional factors will be considered.

Despite the general agreement among documents librarians that the depository library system is a "good" system or that the system is generally "successful" specific criteria for "good" or "successful" are not easily identified. Two broad categories of success that can be suggested are (1) effectiveness, accomplishment of goals and objectives, and (2) efficiency, utilizing the least resources—time, staff, money, etc.—to accomplish those objectives.[6] To examine the effectiveness of the depository system, one must first identify the system's goals and objectives.

Background

A most important beginning point to assess the depository structure is to identify and evaluate its goals and objectives. Goals are different than objectives. Goals may be defined as long range guidelines for organizational or system activities; they suggest general areas that are high priority for the system. Objectives, on the other hand, are short range (one to two years), accomplishable, and measurable statements that describe specific activities to be done during a given period of time.[7] Without meaningful goals and objectives, a system—i.e., a set of interdependent components with a similar purpose—cannot be "successful."[8]

Goals and objectives for the depository library system can be located from two different sources. The statuatory responsibility of the depository system and the system's goal are given in Title 44, Section 1902 of the *U.S. Code*: "government publications, except. . . , shall be made available to depository libraries through the facilities of the Superintendent of Documents for public information." A second source of depository "objectives" can be found in the *Guidelines for the Depository Library System* (1977):[9]

1. The purpose of depository libraries is to make U.S. government publications easily accessible to the general public and to insure their continued availability in the future.
2. The purpose shall be achieved by a system of cooperation wherein depository libraries will receive free federal public documents in return for making them accessible to the general public in their areas.
3. The *Guidelines* are to be considered a recommended level of conduct by all depositories unless otherwise specified by statute or regulations thereunder.

After these preliminary "objectives," specific recommendations are given for various aspects of depository library activities.

Of special interest in the *Guidelines*, are the "Minimum Standards for the Depository Library System," which are listed on the last page and include twelve statements which are given as "standards." Standards may be considered as guidelines that suggest the quality of organizational activities or the quantity of resources necessary to perform these activities. Librarians have had a strange love affair with professional standards which only recently are being replaced by a more usable concept, i.e., performance measures. The validity of standards such as those suggested in the *Guidelines* are suspect because terms are not defined, quantitative levels of performance are not given, and they rest on the assumption that what is "good" for one depository library is "good" for all depository libraries. Space does not allow time to enter the debate of the usefulness of "standards." However, a summary of the difficulties and problems with the concept have been summarized by McClure[10] and some specific problems regarding standards for depository libraries have been discussed by Reynolds.[11]

These "objectives" and "standards" should serve as a basis for determining the effectiveness of the depository system. Unfortunately, they are poorly defined and inadequately stated, thus, are unable to provide a basis to determine effectiveness of the system. Criteria to judge the validity of an objective are suggested in Figure 3-1. These criteria, when applied against the above stated depository objectives indicate that only in some rare instances do any of the objectives meet more than two-thirds of the criteria. The implications from this assessment are significant. First, any method to determine the effectiveness of the depository structure will be limited because the objectives cannot be used to judge the system's effectiveness. Second, the stated objectives and "standards" are so broad and ill-defined, that they can be interpreted to fit a host of different situations, as the need arises. Thus, objectives and standards that mean anything to everyone really mean nothing.

Figure 3-1: Criteria for Judging the Validity of an Objective*

1. Is it, generally speaking, a guide to action?

2. Does it suggest alternative courses of action?

3. Is it explicit enough to suggest certain types of action?

4. Can it be measured?

5. Is it Time Limited?

6. Is it ambitious enough to be challenging?

7. Does it support both the goals and the philosophy of the governing institution?

8. Is the objective coordinated with other objectives and organizational goals so as not to be in conflict with them?

9. Is the objective understood and accepted by individuals who will be responsible for implementing it?

10. Is the objective feasible, that is, are there adequate resources available for its accomplishment?

*Adapted, in part, from: Granger, Charles H. "The Hierarchy of Objectives, Harvard Business Review 42 (May-June, 1964): 64-65.

Another consideration important to evaluating or re-designing the structure of the depository system is to identify existing weakness with the system. The weaknesses of the system related to individual depository libraries (both selective and regional) can be summarized as:

1. lack of adequate support from the host institution in terms of personnel, physical facilities, and budget;
2. frequently, poorly trained staff working as documents librarians;
3. lack of "programming techniques" to promote and integrate documents into the library/community;
4. limited bibliographic control over material;
5. item selection is seen as "collection development"; and
6. ineffective use of technology for improved services.

Additional weakness of the depository library system that are related to the GPO include the following:

1. selection of "high quality" vs. "low quality" documents is difficult because of item number grouping;
2. limited promotion and marketing of depository services and importance of government publications;
3. lack of an effective inspection program based on measurable objectives;
4. uneven distribution of depository library status between academic and public libraries (67 percent academic, 22 percent public, and 11 percent other);[12]
5. access to depository materials primarily through academic and public libraries; other avenues of distribution are ignored;
6. depository status is tied primarily to congressional districts;
7. role of the GPO as a congressional agency limits effectiveness to other governmental agencies as well as individuals seeking information;
8. no unified bibliographic control or access to all government publications; and
9. limited direction and control over depository system activities by system participants.

The lack of meaningful objectives for the depository library system is directly related to the difficulty one encounters in assessing the system's overall effectiveness and its efficiency. Further, the above described weaknesses with the system can be traced, in large part, to the ambiguity of the system's objectives, its overall purposes, and the specific roles that the GPO, the Joint Committee on Printing, the depositories, and other federal information agencies play in the distribution, bibliographic control, and access to government information.[13] Although some of the above weaknesses can be classified as functional problems with the system, it is likely that structural considerations may address and resolve some of them. But, before structural assessment can be meaningfully initiated, two critical assumptions under which the depository system operates must be identified and assessed.

Critical Assumptions

Two critical assumptions regarding the purpose of the depository library system must be clarified, and agreed upon before a depository structure can be evaluated as either "appropriate" or "inappropriate." Figure 3-2 summarizes the two sets of assumptions. The first assumption relates to the definition government information resources. Only a small portion of all government publications enter the depository system as it is currently operated. Depending on how one chooses to define the term government information resources, and the breadth of those resources that might enter the depository system, the structure of the system will be affected.

The second assumption has to do with the administrative control of the system. This administrative control ranges between highly centralized, i.e., the government or some agency of the government retains the authority to direct and enforce the regulations regarding the operation of the system; or, highly decentralized, i.e., the individual depository libraries (or whatever unit at the local level) retains significant control over their specific activities and has the authority to respond to the environment without direction or interference from the government.

These assumptions should not be seen as "either-or" conditions; rather they are scales between the poles of centralized vs. decentralized, and broad concept of government information vs. narrow concept of government information. Depending on the designated purpose of the system, the depository system could fall into one of the four quadrants suggested in Figure 3-2. Generally, the existing depository system falls into quadrant IV: centralized administrative control with a rather narrow concept of government information resources. More importantly, however, is that the existing system falls into this quadrant by default due to lack of clear direction and objectives rather than some preconceived and developing perspective on the role of the depository system.

Identifying these assumptions and determining the "appropriate" degree of centralization vs. de-centralization as well as broad vs. narrow concept of government information resources is critical. Indeed, the recent discussions related to the revision of Title 44 center primarily around these two assumptions.[14] The implications of the assumptions in terms of the four basic quadrants they represent are suggested in Figure 3-3. Each quadrant suggests an impact on the depository structure and may or may not assist the accomplishment of specific system-wide objectives—assuming such objectives can be stated.

A number of performance criteria can be suggested. A performance criterion is a specific result, activity, or expense that affects the overall effectiveness of the system. These performance criteria are ones that many document librarians and government officials discuss in other

Figure 3-2: Critical Assumptions Underlying the Depository System

ADMINISTRATIVE CONTROL

	Decentralized	Centralized
CONCEPT OF GOVERNMENT INFORMATION RESOURCES Broad	I	III
Narrow	II	IV

Centralization: The degree to which administrative control is retained by the highest hierarchical level in the system

Concept of Government Information Resources: The range of government agency publications that are entered into the system

41

Figure 3-3: Implications of Centralization and Concept of Government Information Resources on Selected Criteria

CRITERIA \ QUADRANT	I. BROAD DECENTRALIZED	II. NARROW DECENTRALIZED	III. BROAD CENTRALIZED	IV. NARROW CENTRALIZED
Public Access to Information	HIGH	LOW	MODERATE	VERY LOW
Ability to Encourage Inter-Institutional Cooperation	VERY LOW	MODERATE	LOW	HIGH
System Personnel Requirements	VERY HIGH	MODERATE	MODERATE	VERY LOW
Local Control over Collections	HIGH	LOW	LOW	LOW
System Administrative Expenses	VERY HIGH	MODERATE	HIGH	LOW
Ability to Adapt / Change	VERY LOW	LOW	MODERATE	HIGH
Degree of Bibliographic Control	VERY LOW	LOW	MODERATE	HIGH
Local Space, Personnel, Equipment, & Resources Req'd	VERY HIGH	HIGH	MODERATE	LOW

contexts of depository system operations; however, these—as well as others—can be used to suggest how the various quadrants impact differently on them. In short, the decision as to how the assumptions are to be defined will force the depository system into one of the four quadrants. Depending on the quadrant, the depository system, then, can be expected to be impacted along the broad lines suggested in Figure 3-3.

For example, the performance criterion, public access to information, will have different measures of effectiveness based on whether the structure of the system is centralized-decentralized or government information resources are broadly/narrowly defined. A subjective analysis of the impact of these quadrants on the performance criterion is suggested in the matrix. As can be seen with the criterion public access to information, the range of impacts— from very low access, to high access—is significant.

This figure is presented to indicate the importance of clarifying the assumptions under which the system is to operate. As demonstrated in Figure 3-3, each quadrant represents a number of trade-offs when compared to other quadrants. This concept of trade-offs is most important when considering the structure of the depository system. Furthermore, those individuals involved in the revision of Title 44 or otherwise concerned about improving the effectiveness of the depository system may wish to determine first, the levels of acceptable performance on the criteria suggested in Figure 3-3 *before* an *a priori* decision is made as how best to define the assumptions of centralization and the concept of government information resources.

Importance of Performance Measures

The two assumptions discussed in the previous section suggest the importance of knowing, in advance, what is to be expected from the system. Until those expectations are generally agreed upon, the system will continue to be "all things to all people." And although these assumptions affect both the structure and function of the depository system, no existing criteria have been developed to determine the effectiveness and efficiency of the depository system. Thus, any analysis of the existing depository system must take into consideration the need for clear criteria to determine the effectiveness and efficiency of the system. Poorly constructed and non-measurable objectives for the system exacerbates the problem.

A measure is a means to quantify the object or process in accordance with a rule or procedure that can be used consistently. Without measures, especially performance measures, no valid basis exists to change or restructure a process. Development of such measures calls for concentrated research. Further, Kaplan points out that:

whether we can measure something depends, not on that thing, but on how we have conceptualized it, on our knowledge of it, above all on the skill and ingenuity which we can bring to bear on the process of measurement...[15]

Regardless of perceived difficulties related to establishing performance measures for the depository system, such measures are critically needed.

Performance measures are quantitative indicators of a system's ability to accomplish objectives and respond to the needs of individuals using the system. They provide a basis to evaluate the system and its components, and to develop an ongoing planning process to improve the system. Research into the development of performance measures for the depository library system is non-existant. Despite this dearth of information about how to evaluate the system, there has been no shortage of suggestions for how the system can be changed or modified.

System thinking provides a powerful basis by which one can develop possible performance criteria for the depository library system. Figure 3-4 presents a summary of nine open system characteristics, their definitions, and potential areas for performance measures of the depository system. This listing of possible areas for performance measures is only cursory; additional measures can be suggested for all of the characteristics identified. As the Figure indicates, performance measures for the depository library system can be developed. For example, a number of other areas in library/information science have progressed significantly in developing such performance measures: public library services by DeProspo[16] and Schrader;[17] evaluation of information systems and services by Lancaster[18] and Mick;[19] and networking by Rouse[20] and Williams;[21] to name but a few.

Open systems characteristics are especially important when evaluating the depository library system because they suggest not only possible areas for performance measures but possible structures that will enable the system to better achieve its objectives. Still, an evaluation of the depository system based on open system characteristics contains certain assumptions: first, the system is comprised of interdependent parts, each part has an effect on the other parts; second, the sum of its parts is more than the whole—there is an intangible "essence" of the system that results from the interaction of these parts; and third, system components respond to the environment on a logical and orderly basis—although we may not know what that basis is.[22] Although systems thinking has been around for quite some time, its use as a conceptual basis for the formal evaluation of the depository library system appears not to have been considered.

In answer to the question, on what basis can performance measures be selected to evaluate the depository system, Figure 3-5 is suggested. The specific criteria: appropriateness, informativeness, validity, reproducibility,

Figure 3-4: Depository Evaluation Criteria from Open System Characteristics*

CHARACTERISTIC	POSSIBLE AREAS FOR PERFORMANCE MEASURES
1. Importation of energy-a system functions by importing energy (information, products, materials, etc.) from the larger environment.	Resource Allocation Techniques Relationship between Resources and Goals
2. Throughput-systems move energy through them, largely in the form of transformation processes. These are often multiple processes (decisions, material manipulation, etc.).	Efficiency of processes Decision Analysis Cost/Benefit of Alternatives
3. Output-systems send energy back to the larger environment in the form of products, services, and other kinds of outputs that may be intended or not.	Accomplishment of Objectives Impact of outputs on Environment Appropriateness of Outputs
4. Cycles of events over time-systems function over time and thus are dynamic in nature. Events tend to occur in natural repetitive cycles of input, throughput, and output with events in sequence occurring repeatedly.	Trend data of outputs Flowcharting Degree of Programmed Decision Making
5. Equilibrium seeking-systems tend to move toward the state where all components are in equilibrium, where a steady state exists. When changes are made that result in an imbalance, different components of the system move to restore the balance.	Impact of one component on System at large Comparisons among system components
6. Feedback-systems use information about their output to regulate their input and transformation processes. These informational connections also exist between system components, and thus changes in the functioning of one component lead to changes in other system components (second-order effects).	Mechanisms for Summative and Formative Evaluation System Change over Time Self-Assessment Methods
7. Increasing differentiation-as systems grow, they also tend to increase their differentiation; more components are added, with more feedback loops and more transformation processes. Thus as systems get larger, they also get more complex.	Political relationships among System Components Cooperation/Coordination among system components
8. Equifinality-different system configurations may lead to the same end point, or conversely, the same end state may be reached by a variety of different processes.	Ability of match individual strength to system requirements Comparisons with Depository Competitors
9. System survival requirements-because of the inherent tendency of systems to "run down" or dissipate their energy, certain functions must be performed (at least at minimal levels) over time. These requirements include: (a) goal achievement and (b) adaptation (the ability to maintain balanced successful transactions with the environment).	Interactions with governing board/institutions Response to Environmental demands Ability to identify and obtain new resources

*From Edward Lawler, III, et. al, Organizational Assessment (New York: John Wiley, 1980), p. 267.

comparability, practicality, and input for decision making suggest what one can expect from the measures and can assist researchers to analyze a list of candidate measures and identify those measures that appear to have the greatest potential to evaluate accurately the current operations of the depository system.

By combining the two figures presented in this section, e.g., Depository Evaluation Criteria Based on Open System Characteristics (Figure 3-4) and Criteria to be used in Selecting Measures (Figure 3-5), an important first step can be made to develop meaningful performance measures for the depository library system. Until such measures are developed, depository librarians do not know specific levels of performance that they are expected to fulfill, the Government Printing Office cannot enforce regulations and guidelines realistically, researchers cannot meaningfully evaluate the overall success of the system, and "inspection" of the depository libraries will continue to be little more than a social call from the GPO.[23]

Alternative Depository System Structures

The possible candidates for a depository library structure are limited only to one's imagination, the constraints imposed upon the system by the Government, and the areas for priority activities as depicted in Figure 3-3. Despite these potential constraints, an inspection of the existing system and its functions suggests possible criteria to be considered in the development of an alternative depository structure. Clearly, research is required to determine the appropriateness of these criteria. But possible criteria for the system are:

1. accommodate computerized information processing and other forms of information technology such as satellite and on-line data transmission;
2. provide mechanisms for self-evaluation as well as to demonstrate accountability to outside agencies;
3. coordinate bibliographic control over a broader range of government publications that are "high demand" materials;
4. provide physical and financial resources to assist member libraries/agencies accomplish the goals of the program;
5. provide formal programs of continuing education for depository librarians and certification that such CE has occured;
6. encourage non-library related institutions to serve as "depositories";
7. de-politicize the system by both federal and state governments, i.e., select depository participants by non-governmental agency;
8. promote inter- and intra-institutional cooperation;

Figure 3-5: Criteria to Use in Selecting Measures*

1. <u>Appropriateness</u>: Will it do what I want it to do?

   e.g., "Is it possible to compare the measure across depository libraries?

2. <u>Informativeness</u>: Will it tell me what I need to know?

   e.g., "Will comparing depository libraries of similar size on circulation per capita show which libraries need assistance?"

3. <u>Validity</u>: Does it mean what I think it means?

   e.g., "Is percent of library budget allocated to the documents department a measure of library effectiveness or departmental effectiveness?"

4. <u>Reproducibility</u>: Would someone else get the same answer?

   e.g., "Would two depository librarians reporting on the same library come up with the same score for per-capita use of depository materials?"

5. <u>Comparability</u>: Are we all measuring the same thing?

   e.g, "Do depository libraries in Oklahoma use the same procedures and definitions to count circulation as those in California?"

6. <u>Practicality</u>: Can we afford the time, money, and effort to gather data for this measure?

   e.g., "Is the information gained from the data worth the effort required to determine it?"

7. <u>Input for Decision Making</u>: Will it provide data to assist decision makers?

   e.g., "Is the information likely to identify specific services or operations that can be improved and suggest strategies for their improvement?"

---

*Adapted from R. H. Orr, "Measuring the Goodness of Library Services: A General Framework for Considering Quantitative Measures," <u>Journal</u> <u>of</u> <u>Documentation</u> 29, no. 3 (September, 1973): 315-332.

9. minimize duplication of services provided by the private sector;
10. increase access to government publications by a wider range of user groups; and
11. keep system costs at a minimum.

Development of criteria for an alternative depository system must precede the selection of any structure that may replace the existing one.

While a number of writers have criticized the existing depository library structure, very few specific recommendations have been suggested to replace it. During the recent discussions surrounding the possible revision of Title 44, at hearings regarding structural changes, Public Printer John J. Boyle stated:

...it may be worth considering separating the Superintendent of Documents Operation from the Government Printing Office, leaving the GPO where it is, and establishing Documents as a separate agency in the Executive Branch with a Commission to determine policy for broader dissemination of government information...The cataloging and indexing function of the Documents department, albeit very important, could be located anywhere in government without destroying its effectiveness.[24]

Such suggestions are worth careful scrutiny. Indeed, alternative structural changes in the depository system have not been formally compared and evaluated. The system continues to operate largely on the assumptions on which it was created—many of which simply are no longer valid given the changes in our society, the technological advances in information processing, and the changing view of the role of the Federal government vis-a-vis the private citizen.

Given the limitations under which any depository structure evaluation must occur, the criteria suggested earlier for the development of candidate depository structures, and the changing assumptions under which the system must operate, a number of alternative structures can be identified. The following alternative structures are not intended to be comprehensive proposals for a modified structure nor are they intended to be "blue-sky" suggestions. Rather, they are put forward to compare to the existing structure, to present ideas that can be incorporated into the system, and to encourage more research to compare possible alternatives critically, and formally evaluate the relative effectiveness and efficiency of the alternative structures.

The Existing Structure. Currently, the depository system operates on a clear hierarchy in which local depositories report through regional depositories (with limited resources and authority) to the Superintendent of

Documents. The Superintendent of Documents is but one portion of the Government Printing Office which has additional responsibilities but limited powers of enforcement and a narrow perspective of "government publications" that eventually enter the depository system. Detailed description of the structure and existing responsibilities can be found in the most recent *U.S. Government Manual.*[25]

The Centralized Agency Approach. This alternative structure would combine all government printing activities into one central agency that had responsibility for acquisition, organization, bibliographic control, printing, and dissemination of the broad range of government publications and coordinating existing publication activities among an host of agencies such as NTIS, ERIC, Department of Energy, and many more. Given this centralization of publication activities, either the existing depository structure could be used or depository structures from some of the alternatives listed below could be combined with the approach.

Information Resource Center Approach. This approach would encourage the establishment of smaller depository collections of less than 25 percent item selection. These information resource centers (IRC) would not have the same regulations as regionals or selective depository libraries, thus, they would be better able to address unique information needs of specific clientele. They could be established in public, school, or special libraries. Such an approach would assist to increase access to government publications to a wider audience and assist the depositories that did not wish to obtain a large percentage of the items. Hernon has discussed this approach in greater detail elsewhere.[26]

Area Regional Depository Approach. Much controversy exists as to the role and effectiveness of the existing regional depository structure; indeed, during the early discussion of revising Title 44, the regional structure was eliminated.[27] An area regional approach would maintain the concept of the regional as an intermediary to assist the local depositories or IRCs but would reduce their number from approximately 40 to no more than ten or fourteen (corresponding to GPO regional printing plants). These regionals would have responsibility for a broader geographic area, and would be subsidized in part by the central publication agency to perform specific activities including instruction, inspection, collection development, networking and cooperation, sales, and perhaps additional responsibilities.

The Voucher Approach. This approach would utilize a system whereby government publications would be sent only to those libraries or other public agencies where individuals had submitted vouchers from the government for purchasing documents. In such an approach, only those agencies where people actually utilized government materials would the agency get "free" materials from the government. Such an approach would greatly reduce the costs of operating the existing system—one in which some librarians believe that upwards to 50 percent of all depository items are not circulated after receipt. Local depositories and IRCs could, of course, purchase whatever they choose, or might be given an allocation of vouchers to assist in overall collection development.

The Commercial Approach. A number of commercial vendors already have depository systems that are available on a "pay as you go" basis. Indeed, microformatted government publications of depository items, congressional materials, statistical information, and others are available on a commercial basis. A structure could be established whereby all distribution of materials would be accomplished by a commercial vendor, either partially supported by the government or by the local libraries and public agencies wishing to collect such materials. In short, the government would hire a commercial firm to provide depository services through any of the other structures suggested in this section.

The Sales/Depository Approach. Instead of the existing system that separates the sales program from the depository program, the two could be combined. Each state might have a central sales office for public access and purchase of materials *and* also be responsible for distributing depository materials to appropriate local agencies. In this approach, the local sales agencies might use a voucher system to obtain the documents from the government, receive specific titles of publications on a depository basis, or simply purchase those items desired. This approach would place greater emphasis on marketing and selling government publications to the public rather than depositing them into what many believe to be archival storage at libraries.

The Approval Plan Approach. Using the commercial vendors, once again, as a model, a structure could be set up whereby local depositories or IRCs develop a profile of their information resource requirements from the government, and then receive regular shipments of government publications that meet those criteria. If materials, once examined in the local agency, do not meet expectations, they can be returned to the central agency for full credit. The structure for this approach could simplify existing depository arrangements with the Federal government by eliminating the role of the regionals and reducing the staff required at the Office of the Superintendent of Documents. Such an approach could be combined with the Commercial approach described above and take the government out of the publication/distribution business.

The State Data Center Approach. One innovative approach to encourage the accessibility of Census materials has been the establishment of State Data Centers. Using this approach as a model, each state could have a Documents Center that not only provided access to all government documents, but had specially trained staff to assist users in accessing the information from the government. In such a structure, the IRCs requiring Federal documents might inspect first, publications prior to purchase, obtain expertise on how to utilize and access the information, and serve as a referral agency to the State Documents Center. The major difference between the existing regional structure and the state data centers is the latter's emphasis on providing information services rather than providing information storage as a major responsibility.

A Comprehensive Approach. Figure 3-6 suggests an alternative depository structure that might best be characterized as a comprehensive approach. It draws on existing federal structures and incorporates a number of characteristics described in the alternative structures above. Major changes from the existing structure are (1) establishing a centralized agency to control and distribute all government publications, (2) encouraging intergovernmental cooperation regarding publication/distribution, (3) creating eight regionals with significantly expanded responsibilities and resource support from the government, (4) providing a formal mechanism to conduct research/development related to government printing and access to government information resources, (5) allowing for an expansion of local public agencies to be part of the system as IRCs without burdening them with regulations to maintain a large collection for a selected clientele, (6) promoting marketing and sales of government publications at a local level, and (7) continuing the policy of developing mechanisms for increased participant interaction and control over the system. Such an approach appears to meet a number of the criteria suggested earlier in the chapter and provides a means that may have potential to improve the effectiveness and efficiency of the system.

The alternative structures suggested are illustrative of possible approaches that could be considered to improve the existing system. Clearly, much more space would be required to detail each approach and critically identify its potential impact on improved services or other criteria that might be suggested. The combinations and variations that could be developed by intermingling the approaches appear to be endless. Presently, rational decision making cannot be easily employed to compare the

Figure 3-6: Alternative Depository Structures: The Comprehensive Approach

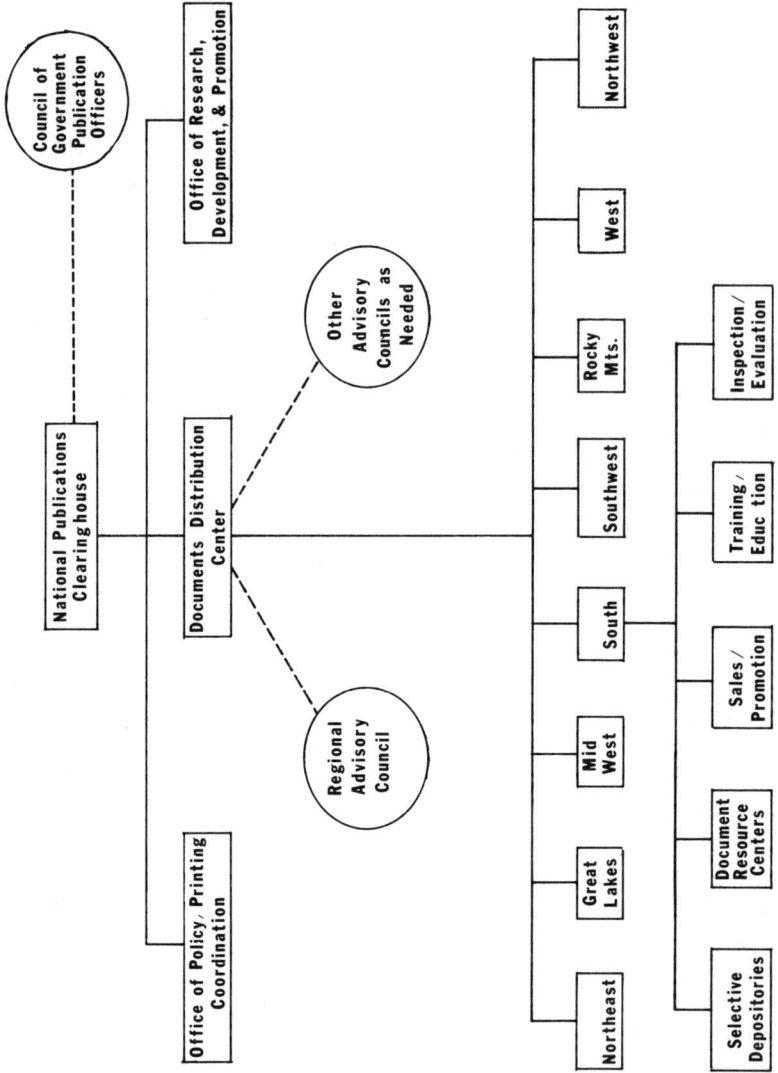

various approaches and determine which has the greatest potential to improve the depository system. Only after clear objectives for a depository system and performance criteria are established can the implications of these candidate structures be meaningfully evaluated.

Moving Toward a Reassessment

This chapter has attempted to identify specific aspects of the depository library system that affect its structure and overall effectiveness. Although the existing structure may provide adequate access and distribution to selected government publications, a number of weaknesses with the structure and function of the system can be identified. These weaknesses suggest specific areas where improvements can be made in the depository library structure.

Perhaps the biggest problem to be resolved is the clarification of the goals and objectives of the depository library system. Existing documentation regarding the depository library system provides neither goals nor objectives but rather some broadly stated purposes and "standards" for the system. This broadness results in considerable ambiguity that hinders the depository system from being either effective or efficient. Indeed, without clearly stated objectives, no realistic measure of effectiveness can be made and specific performance measures are difficult to establish.

The ambiguity over the stated purposes of the depository system is compounded by a lack of Federal definitions regarding underlining assumptions related to the depository system. Until (1) the range of government publications that are to enter the depository system and (2) the degree to which the government will maintain central control over the system are *clearly determined*, everyone will have different expectations from the system in terms of its administration and its outputs. Any changes in the existing structure of the depository system must be preceeded by a definition of these two issues.

Conceptually, the impact of these two assumptions on the structure of the depository system is critical. Depending on the mix between range of publications entering the system and degree of centralization, the impact of proposed depository structures on other criteria related to the system (see Figure 3-3) can change drastically. In short, a design for revamping the depository structure must recognize that trade-offs are likely to occur among the various performance criteria. The conclusion is that designers must first determine the criteria for performance that are to be considered as "most important" and *then* develop a structure that will facilitate "good" or acceptable performance on those criteria.

An assessment of the depository structure suggests that meaningful evaluation will be difficult without the development of performance measures or agreed upon depository performance criteria. Using general systems thinking as a means to facilitate an evaluative design for the system, a number of open systems characteristics suggest specific areas for performance criteria. The development of performance criteria can then serve as a basis to (1) know how well the depository system is operating now, (2) identify specific areas for system improvement, and (3) suggest alternative structures that might better accomplish the depository objectives. Regardless of the depository structure—whether it be the existing one or an alternative one—the development of performance measures is desperately needed.

Given these limitations, the need for a clear understanding of what the depository system is expected to accomplish, and the need to develop performance criteria to determine the effectiveness and efficiency of the system, are needed before alternative depository structures can be suggested. Once again, each of the various alternatives will have strengths and weaknesses; trade-offs must be recognized. However, a rational approach can be used to determine which of the alternatives can best accomplish the objectives of the system and meet specific evaluative criteria that detail the expectations of system administrators and users. Although numerous structures and combinations can be suggested, they must be rationally evaluated in terms of cost, benefits, impacts, and trade-offs. A formal research project is necessary to accomplish such an evaluation.

Such a research project could be encouraged and recommended by the Depository Library Council. Indeed, the Depository Library Council can play an important role to promote the need for such research, encourage the government or private sector to fund research of this nature, and act as an advisory board to such research projects. In short, document librarians must work together to encourage that formally funded research be done on the depository library system; they must bring pressure on the GPO, the professional associations and the Congress, to recognize the need for such research; and they must become more involved in the research process themselves.

The critical issue is the need for decisions related to the depository library structure to be based on research and empirical evidence rather than opinion and politics. Although the depository system clearly is a political entity and thus, is subject to a number of political impacts, the GPO can take a more aggressive stance on obtaining analyses of their operations and use such data as a basis for making specific recommendations regarding the system. One cannot read the recent materials related to the revision of Title 44 without recognizing the lack of factual evidence presented regarding impacts, costs, objectives, and other criteria for the depository structure. Yet, one of the recommendations that was presented would eliminate the regional libraries from the depository structure. The reality simply is that no research has been done to determine if regionals are "effective" or "successful" in meeting objectives. Replacing or restructuring the existing depository structure without a research basis of information is ineffective decision making at best and dangerous to the concept of access to government information at worst. Research studies must replace opinion and untested assumptions.

Thus, the analysis of the depository structure identifies a number of problems—many of which are conceptual and philosophical. But others are simply related to a lack of clear objectives and a paucity of performance measures that identify our expectations from the system. A research agenda regarding the depository structure would include the following:

1. analyze existing strengths and weaknesses based on quantifiable data;
2. establish a short-term and long-term planning process between the government and local depositories;
3. identify alternative depository structures with costs and benefits of each approach;
4. establish performance measures for the various candidate depository structures;
5. present candidate list of goals and objectives to depository decision makers;
6. develop a program for on-going formal planning, review, and evaluation based on goals, objectives, and performance criteria.

With such information in hand, rational decisions can be made to improve the depository system, structures can be devised that best meet the objectives of the system, and citizens' access to and knowledge of government information resources can be increased.

References

1. Morehead, Joe. *Introduction to United States Public Documents*. 2nd ed. (Littleton, CO: Libraries Unlimited, 1978).
2. Buckley, Carper W. "Implementation of the Federal Depository Library Act of 1962," *Library Trends*, 15 (July 1966): 27-36.
3. Schwarzkopf, LeRoy C. "The Depository Library Program and Access by the Public to Official Publications of the United States Government," *Government Publications Review*, 5 (1978): 147-156.
4. *Instructions to Depository Libraries*. Washington: Government Printing Office, Superintendent of Documents, 1977.
5. Dubin, Robert. *Theory Building* (New York: The Free Press, 1969).
6. McClure, Charles R. "Microformatted Government Publications: Planning for the Future," *Government Publications Review*, 5 (1978): 511-515.

7. McClure, Charles R. "The Planning Process: Strategies for Action," *College and Research Libraries*, 39 (November, 1978): 456-466.

8. Churchman, C. West. *The Systems Approach* (New York: Dell, 1966).

9. *Guidelines for the Depository Library System* (Washington, D.C.: Government Printing Office, Superintendent of Documents, 1977).

10. McClure, Charles R. "From Public Library Standards to Development of Statewide Levels of Adequacy," *Library Research*, 2 (1980): 45-46.

11. Reynolds, Catharine J. "Standards for Depository Libraries: Goals and Roadblocks," *Documents to the People*, 4 (March 1976): 45-46.

12. Whitbeck, George W., Peter Hernon, and John Richardson Jr. "The Federal Depository Library System: A Descriptive Analysis," *Government Publications Review*, 5 (1978): 253-267.

13. Richardson, John V., Dennis C. W. Frisch, and Catherine Hall. "Bibliographic Organization of the U.S. Federal Depository Collections," *Government Publications Review*, 7A (1980): 463-480.

14. Schwarzkopf, LeRoy C. "Title 44 Revision," *Documents to the People*, 8 (September, 1980): 228-230.

15. Kaplan, Abraham. *The Conduct of Inquiry: Methodology For Behavioral Science* (Scranton, PA: Chandler Publishing Co., 1964).

16. DeProspo, Ernest R., Ellen Altman, and Kenneth E. Beasley. *Performance Measures for Public Libraries* (Chicago; ALA, 1973).

17. Schrader, Alvin M. "Performance Measures for Public Libraries: Refinements in Methodology and Reporting," *Library Research*, 2 (1980-81): 129-155.

18. Lancaster, F. Wilfrid. *The Measurement and Evaluation of Library Services* (Washington, D.C.: Information Resources Press, 1977).

19. Mick, Colin K. "Cost Analysis of Information Systems and Services," in Martha E. Williams, ed., *Annual Review of Information Science and Technology*, Vol. 14. (White Plains, NY: Knowledge Industries 1979), pp. 36-64.

20. Rouse, William B. and Rouse, Sandra H. *Management of Library Networks* (New York: Wiley, 1980).

21. Williams, J. G. "Performance Criteria and Evaluation for a Library Resource Sharing Network," in *Library Resource Sharing* (New York: Marcel Dekker, 1977), pp. 225-277.

22. Churchman, C. West. *The Systems Approach and Its Enemies* (New York: Basic Books, 1979).

23. McClure, Charles R. "Opinion: GPO Inspection Program," *Government Publications Review*, 8 (1980): 450-452.

24. U.S. Congress. House. Committee on House Administration, Subcommittee on Printing. *The National Publications Act*. Hearing, 96th Congress, 1st Session on H.R. 5424 to amend Title 44, United States Code, November 14, 1979. (Washington, D.C.: Government Printing Office, 1979).

25. *U.S. Government Manual 1980-1981* (Washington, D.C.: Government Printing Office, 1980).

26. Hernon, Peter. *Microforms and Government Information* (Westport, CN: Microform Review, 1981).

27. U.S. Congress. House. *National Publications Act of 1979*. H.R. 5424. 96th Congress, 1st Session.

THE USES AND MISUSES OF INFORMATION FOUND IN GOVERNMENT PUBLICATIONS

By Joe Morehead

Introduction

Once upon a time, when I worked at the reference desk of the documents department of a large, metropolitan public library, a man whose visage and demeanor I came to know well appeared every Friday morning and, in a blunt and businesslike manner, asked for the 7 or 8 current issues of "FT-410." While the page was retrieving the issues from the stacks, he had already staked out a desk in the reference room and was poised, pencil and notepad in hand, by the time the issues were delivered. He would spend anywhere from an hour to two hours studying FT-410 with awesome concentration. Then he would get up, return the issues to the desk, and depart.

As many of you know, FT-410 is one of those innumerable Census Bureau periodicals covering commodity groupings of U.S. exports, the issuing provenance being the Foreign Trade Division of the Bureau. After a while, my colleagues and I looked forward to the punctual visits of this austere gentleman. Since this was all he ever requested in the documents department, he became known as "dear old FT-410." I often wondered what he used those arcane statistics for, these data that somehow escaped my academic concerns as a philosophy and literature major. Was Mr. FT-410 using the data to consummate ineffably risky and prosperous ventures? Did he represent a company (as many of our patrons did) or was he running his own business? Or was he just another of the many eccentric customers who wandered into the library, getting his kicks reading export statistics? If this activity could be endowed with romance and adventure, we found imaginative release in speculating about the user needs of one of our favorite patrons.

When I was asked to speak at this conference on the user and public access to government information, I cast about for an aspect of the topic that has not been as prominently discussed in our profession as other facets of the problem, and somehow the picture of Mr. FT-410 kept recurring as a paradigm. We have spent much time and effort—rightly so, I believe—on the problems of lack of access to the government publications we ought to have—more committee prints, Non-GPO publications, and the like. We have spent time and effort on improving the bibliographical control over government materials. We have analyzed the many problems of organization and management, of segregated vs. integrated collections, of microform use, of depository systems, of cataloging and classifying. But what I have always been interested in is the use of all this government information to its manifold consumers: government itself, the private sector, the academic community, individuals like Mr. FT-410.

When we address a problem like user access, at least four components can be readily identified:

1. Government information must be reasonably easy to obtain physically; that is, by means of a nearby depository library, through the mails, or whatever—within a reasonable amount of time.

2. Government information must be reasonably easy to obtain bibliographically. This involves a psychological dimension. Studies have shown that seekers of information will give up if the search for verification and location consumes too much time and effort.

3. Government information must be reasonably inexpensive or free— at least free to use in a library.

4. Government information, once found, must be reasonably accurate; moreover, we want our users to *interpret* government information with care and accuracy.

The first three components that I mentioned quite correctly continue to occupy our theoretical and practical concerns. But when I used to observe Mr. FT-410 pouring over his monthly export statistics, it never occured to me that his evident concentration and dedication might not involve a knowledgeable assessment of the reliability of the data he perused. In short, I did not think about the problem at all. I was pleased to know enough to retrieve the information for him, and that was the end of my professional responsibility. Had the patron been a junior high-school student on an assignment to write something about United States exports, I would have questioned his use of FT-410 and nudged him toward the *World Book Encyclopedia*. But the question arises: should the reference librarian be trained to advise the adult user about the reliability of government information? My feeling is that for some types of government information, which are so clearly disposed to incorrect inferences by the unsophisticated user, the librarian ought to be acquainted with the problems and pitfalls—at least in a general way. Since no one can be a subject specialist for all the areas of information produced or disseminated by governments, the acquiring of a second master's degree or even a doctorate is not really a solution. For it seems to me that the bottom line of all our efforts to provide access is simply this: that our users, if at all possible, come away with trustworthy information that they will use in a responsible manner.

The dubious legitimacy of information that appears in government publications covers so many categories that I have chosen to limit my remarks to three areas with which I have some familiarity. These categories assume national importance. They have explosive political, economic, and social consequences. They are constantly in the news. And they have been, and continue to be, the focus of a great deal of scholarly commentary and analysis. I am speaking of (1) crime data supplied by the Uniform Crime Reporting Program and by Victimization Surveys; (2) statistics supplied by the Bureau of Labor Statistics on the volatile and urgent problems of consumer prices, unemployment, and the like; and (3) the dissemination of energy information—oil and gas resources and reserves and related energy matters.

Crime Reporting

The New York Times recently carried a news item in which these words were stated: "According to the F.B.I.'s Uniform Crime Reports, violent crime rose 47.3 percent during the 1970's." One of the several problems we encounter when we read something like this is the insidious and almost subliminal appeal to the authoritative nature of statistical pronouncements. The culprit here is the ".3" in the figure. It suggests that crime rates over a decade can be measured accurately down to a tenth of a percentage point. It implies that the compiler of this datum has found a methodology of surgical precision. And it implies that the surrounding words and thoughts are as impressively exact as the number. All such implications are unjustified.

Ironically, the more precise the figures given, the more we tend to believe them. Because we worship statistics as much as we misuse them, all of this sounds very professional and correct. The consumer of this piece of information may act upon the presumed reliability of the figure in several ways: by writing an indignant letter to some official; by voting for a candidate who has vowed to reduce or reverse this appalling trend; by purchasing a sophisticated lock and alarm system for his or her home; by going out and buying a handgun for protection.

The FBI has been issuing so-called "uniform crime data" since 1930. We may obtain them in depository libraries or through the SuDocs sales office annually as "Crime in the United States," but virtually all who use these data or write about them employ the series acronym UCR. How does the UCR program work, that it can come up with such a precise figure as "47.3"?

Some 15,000 law enforcement agencies throughout the country submit their statistics either directly to the FBI or through state uniform crime reporting programs. Offenses are divided into 8 serious categories called "Crime Index" offenses and 22 categories of so-called "less serious" offenses excluding minor traffic violations. The "Crime Index" offenses are those that arouse the emotions of fear and anger: murder, robbery, rape, arson, burglary, assault, and so on. Local police data are collected by the FBI. They are edited, correlated, manipulated, analyzed and computerized to produce a myriad of charts, tables and graphs. One of the features of the UCR annual reports is a "Crime Clock" illustrating the frequency of major offenses. The most recent Clock shows that, for example, one "Crime Index" offense was committed every three seconds, one violent crime every 30 seconds, and so on: a graphic and frightening depiction. Yet other tables in the UCR show that homicide, for example, represents less than one percent and all violent crimes less than ten percent of total "Crime Index" offenses. While the "Crime Clock" gives the impression that most crime is of a violent nature, other UCR data provide a different perspective.

Indeed, throughout the UCR caveats abound regarding the interpretation of the crime data set forth. For example, both the FBI and scholars have insisted that we must not compare the statistical information of one individual community with that of another. For instance, cities with excellent police-community relations tend to have a *high* rate of crime reporting by citizens. But this fact has not dampened the enthusiasm of the news media for glibly designating a particular city each year as the "Crime Capital" of the Nation. Here is, alas, an altogether too typical instance of a "user" of government information—namely, the news media, —misinterpreting that information. And how many of us rely in large measure upon the media for our information about society?

Newspaper, radio and TV distortion aside, the UCR suffer from many limitations. For one thing, crime estimates are *lower* than actual frequency. Not all local law enforcement agencies report to the FBI. Some police departments do not follow the definitions of crime categories, hence there is less "uniformity" than desired. And some police agencies, for political or other pressures, report information to the UCR that is totally unlike that which appears in their own files.

VICTIMIZATION SURVEYS

In 1972 the now defunct Law Enforcement Assistance Administration (LEAA), with the help of the Census Bureau, instituted the National Crime Surveys (NCS). They have aroused interest by their contrast with official UCR figures, and provide an alternative or supplement to FBI reported crime data. Because NCS figures project almost twice as much "actual" crime as the annual UCR data, the latter information is made to seem even more disreputable than skeptics had been proclaiming.

But NCS annual reports, called *Criminal Victimization in the United States* (also a depository item and a sales publication), are household surveys of a representative national sample; interviews are conducted with thousands of occupants of housing units. NCS statistics, for example, include crimes not reported to the police as well as those reported. And they differ in several other methodological respects from UCR. Yet the urge to compare NCS and UCR data has been beyond the self-control of those users who make commenting on crime figures a hobby or a business.

An obvious advantage of NCS methodology is the revelation of the substantial number of crimes that are not reported to the police. But as criminal justice researchers began to evaluate NCS techniques, they found problems in the methodology of this effort at enumerating crime. For one thing, information given by respondents bears a large margin of error: memory failures about when crimes occurred, and even outright prefabrication exists. Moreover, interviewers and coders tend to skew the data toward a showing of greater criminality than was actually the case, owing to organizational pressures. Unfortunately, NCS figures have spawned almost as much disaffection as UCR data.

I will not even attempt to discuss the immense methodological problems associated with the analysis of the scope of *organized crime* or that pervasive category called "white collar crime." The best that scholars can say about UCR and NCS statistics is that they provide a rough portrait of the directional nature of specific offense patterns, which suggest more appropriate strategies for law enforcement organizations. The irony of these crime data is that we have more accurate information about the way they are misused by the news media and cynical politicians than we do about the magnitude of crime itself. We also know that, despite half a century of UCR figures and numerous attempts to refine the methodology, there still exists the presence of error of considerable proportions.

BLS STATISTICS

Ranking closely behind the Census Bureau in the amount of statistical activity is the Bureau of Labor Statistics of the Labor Department. It generates a multitude of data on such crucial aspects of our economy as wholesale prices, consumer prices, unemployment, work stoppages, productivity and costs, and many other series. These figures appear in monthly, quarterly or annual publications, most of which are available to depository libraries or by sales subscriptions. When figures are released on a specific indicator each month, the coverage in the news media is swift and solemn. Indeed, the arithmetic involved causes tremors in the body politic and affects elections. A Gallup poll in 1976 indicated that the electorate, by a two to one margin, believed that the Democrats were most likely to restore the nation's prosperity. The fear of unemployment outweighed the perils of inflation: by voting "their pocketbooks," the masses were said to have tilted the election to Jimmy Carter. Four years later, there is little doubt that inflation, as well as unemployment, contributed significantly to Ronald Reagan's victory.

Of all the statistical series issued by the BLS, two have particular social volatility, and I would like to comment on them.

EMPLOYMENT

Once a month the Bureau issues a press release called "The Employment Situation" which shows a variety of employment/unemployment rates and indicators. Later this information shows up in a monthly called *Employment and Earnings*—a depository item and a SuDocs sales periodical. What everyone looks at in this mass of statistics is the rate of unemployment. This percentage shows that portion of the labor force that is actively seeking work but cannot find it. BLS statisticians are very sophisticated people, however. They publish numerous articles in government periodicals and commerical journals that demonstrate several alternate ways in which the rate of unemployment can be measured. Indeed, the present formula has been criticized by the head of BLS himself. The current rate does not, for instance, measure those who have become too discouraged to seek employment, nor does it measure those who are "underemployed." Black teenage unemployment has always shown terribly high rates, but some economists believe this is related to an artificially high minimum wage law.

The statistics themselves reveal curious patterns. It is possible in a given month to have the unemployment rate rise at the same time the number of jobholders in the country rises. The summer months release students into the labor force and this affects the rate. Unemployment benefits in many industries are said to create "disincentives" to seek other jobs. All of these factors are well documented by footnotes and small-print commentary. But, unhappily, the raw figure is the one that grabs headlines and triggers political activity that may not be helpful in the long run.

When consumers of this kind of government information, abetted by the news media, seize upon the overall unemployment rate without considering other factors readily available in the statistical tables, they are misusing government information. When the BLS suggests a change in the method of measuring unemployment—a change that would show a *lower* rate—the cry of political meddling is heard in the land. If the formula were changed to show a *greater* rate of unemployment, the party in power would swiftly see to it that the Commissioner of Labor Statistics was no longer in the employ of the government.

In fact, BLS statisticians have devised no fewer than *seven* measures of unemployment, designated U-1 through U-7, and these series are regularly published in tabular form. The U-1 ratio measures persons unemployed 15 weeks or longer as a percent of the civilian labor force. The U-7 measure includes total full-time jobseekers, plus ½ part-time jobseekers, plus ½ total on part time for economic reasons, plus discouraged workers as a percent of the civilian labor force, plus discouraged workers less ½ of the part-time labor force. As we measure from U-1 to U-7, the rate of unemployment grows progressively worse. According to the January 1981, "Employment Situation" (released February 6, 1981), U-1 measured a benign 2.2 percent unemployment rate while U-7 measured over 10 percent. Our official rate is a middle ground, called U-5, and is defined as "total unemployed as a percent of the civilian labor force." Currently it stands at 7.4 percent and includes anyone who is not employed but who made specific efforts to find employment sometime during the preceding 4 weeks.

If we had been using the measures of unemployment devised for Great Britain, it is safe to say that the political landscape over the last years would have been strewn with different corpses. In Great Britain, unemployment is based on the actual number of persons who take the trouble to go to government facilities and register themselves as being out of work and wanting a job. Economists have estimated that British unemployment rates, if they were calculated using our official U-5 definition, would be approximately *twice* as high as they are in the official British reports. This is something to bear in mind when you read about the economic vicissitudes of the Thatcher government. In the past, when Great Britain enjoyed sunnier days on the economic scene, we heard numerous self-appointed gurus of the political arena making invidious comparisons between the level of unemployment of the two countries. Of course these "experts" were comparing apples and oranges, and by so doing were misusing government information.

Although these nuances are available to any user of government information who takes the trouble to locate them, most people are likely to be swayed by the now legendary maxim that goes: "When my neighbor is out of work, it's a recession; when I'm out of a job, it's a depression." And it is this emotion, not the sophisticated subtleties of statistical manipulation, that translates into political activity, media coverage, and electoral patterns.

CONSUMER PRICES

The Consumer Price Index (CPI) is another monthly package of information that causes convulsions in the body politic. Many of you subscribe to this monthly (which is called the *CPI Detailed Report*), along with a companion periodical, *Producer Prices and Price Indexes* (formerly called the *Wholesale Price Index*).

The CPI measures the price change of a constant market basket of goods and services over a period of time. One use of it, therefore, is as an index of price change. During periods of rising prices (which in recent years has been continual), it is an index of inflation and is used to measure the success or failure of government economic policy.

Another major use of the CPI is to escalate income payments. More than 8½ million workers are covered by collective bargaining contracts which provide for increases in wage rates based on increases in the CPI. It has thus become a powerful tool in drafting new contracts and in wage negotiations. In addition, various federal statutes mandate adjustments in wages and benefits as the CPI rises: About 31 million social security beneficiaries, about 2½ million retired military and federal civil service employees and survivors, about 20 million food stamp recipients, and almost 25 million children who eat lunch at school under the National School Lunch Act and the Child Nutrition Act. The CPI also affects the official definition of poverty, which becomes the basis of eligibility in numerous health and welfare programs at the federal, state, and local government level.

Despite the tremendous impact of the CPI, most consumers of this information relate only to the bottom line. The layperson rarely questions the reliability of the monthly figures. But the way in which the CPI has been constructed over the years has involved changes in methodology. The CPI began during World War I (then called the "cost-of-living" index, a term still used by newscasters) as a way of determining a fair wage scale for the shipbuilding industry. In 1921 the CPI was issued quarterly; it became a monthly in 1940. It has undergone major revisions in methodology since then: 1953, 1964, and most recently in 1978. Each revision has been called an "improvement" by the BLS.

With all these improvements, the BLS admits that the determination of just who should make up the index population is still a major problem. When a blue-ribbon panel recently recommended that the index reflect groups other than simply urban wage earners and clerical workers, the AFL-CIO objected strenuously, fearing that it would hurt collective bargaining. The BLS finds it very difficult to isolate a segment of the population that is both large enough to encompass most current uses of the index and narrow enough to be considered homogeneous in reflecting price experience. The compromise is the devising of a "family of indexes," roughly analogous to the array of unemployment data released by the BLS. Thus organized labor could have its own index for bargaining, non-unionized workers their own index, and so on.

Accordingly, since January, 1978, the Bureau has been publishing CPI's for two population groups: (1) A *new CPI* for all urban consumers, which covers approximately 80 percent of the total noninstitutional civilian population, and (2) a *revised CPI* for urban wage earners and clerical workers, which represents about 50 percent of the new CPI. This new index includes groups which historically have been excluded from CPI coverage, such as professional, managerial and technical workers, the self-employed, short-term workers, the unemployed, retirees, and others not in the labor force. Price changes for various items are averaged together with weights that represent their importance in the spending of the appropriate population group.

A number of scholars have charged that the CPI is upwardly biased and therefore overstates the impact of inflation in reducing real earnings. They cite the fact that the CPI has fixed weights and thus does not account for substitution effects induced by changes in relative prices. They point out that the CPI cannot adequately reflect quality improvements, innovations, and new products. They complain that, in recent times, house purchases are treated in the same manner as other durable goods; because house prices have increased substantially relative to other prices, the inclusion of this statistic has had a significant impact in pushing up the overall index. This housing indicator, in fact, has generated such widespread criticism that in January 1981, the Commissioner of Labor Statistics announced that the home-purchase component would be eliminated and replaced with a "rental equivalency" statistic—that is, a BLS estimate of how much home owners would have to pay if they were renting their houses. Indeed, the Bureau was prepared to make such a change in the mid-1970s for the major CPI revision of 1978. But organized labor lobbied vociferously to oppose the change, and the Carter administration acquiesed.

Organized labor had reason for its opposition. Rapidly rising real estate prices and home loan interest rates exaggerate the rise of the CPI, whereas a "rental equivalency" figure is likely to rise less rapidly. Critics of the current measure point out that very few consumers make such a purchase in any given month, thus the population sample is unreliably low. In addition, buying a house is more appropriately defined as an "investment item" rather than a "consumption item."

But the change to a rental equivalency figure will not take place until the next major revision of the CPI in 1985. When it does, the *Index* is expected to show a decrease in the rise of the overall price level, and that will mean smaller pay increases for those constituencies that are tied by law or contract to the CPI. Until 1985, however, home purchases will continue to contribute to rising CPI.

The BLS would prefer to produce its various analyses in an atmosphere free from the impure air of political pressures; but, alas, this is not possible. However, any changes in CPI measurements must, by definition, change the overall index *rate*. And this is an emotional issue with enormous political consequences. Even a slight change in the figures— fractions of a percent—involves millions and millions of dollars gained or lost in wages, social security benefits, food stamp programs, and a host of other federal health and welfare measures.

The irony of CPI statistics is that the interpretations assigned to the information are by no means the most reliable measure of the impact of inflation on disposable income. Economists have demonstrated that "real" prices for many items are lower today than they were twenty-five years ago. By comparing the number of hours one had to work to obtain goods at a particular time in history, experts have found that an hour of work in 1979 actually bought 15 percent more in goods and services than it did in 1955. And this relative measure even applies to those items we find most to complain about—clothing, apartments, rentals, health care, even gasoline. Thus by taking another BLS series of hourly after-tax wages and combining them with CPI data we may reach a totally different picture than that realized from CPI data alone.

With FBI crime statistics, unemployment data, cost-of-living figures, indeed with all studies involving the use of numbers, one must be aware that changes occur over time and that multivariable constructs yield better inferences than the individual components of those constructs allow. And one must know that any statistical construct is an imperfect representation of reality; it is shaped by the process which operationally defines it, the procedures which capture it, and the organization which processes and interprets it. But because such information appears between the covers of a government publication, many users attribute to it the power and value of holy writ.

Energy Information

I have saved the most egregious example for last. On October 19, 1973, the Arab oil-producing nations imposed a total ban on oil exports to the United States, and this ban was not lifted until March 18, 1974. Remember the long gas lines, the rumors of a vast, despicable conspiracy between the huge transnational oil companies and the oil producers, the rapidly rising prices of gasoline and home heating oil, the panicky reaction of the Congress as hearings and inquiries were convened, the feeling of helplessness?

It was during this time that many people became aware of an interesting aspect of information disseminated by the federal government. For years, the government had been relying solely upon the periodic estimates of oil and natural gas reserves compiled by the American Petroleum Institute (API) and the American Gas Association (AGA). And the government had not been doing this in some clandestine fashion. All we had to do was look at the introductory remarks or footnotes in any number of reference sources issued by the Bureau of Mines, the US Geological Survey, and the several other agencies that published this information. I recall helping patrons find information in such venerable publications as the 4-volume *Minerals Yearbook*. But when I pointed out the source notes to the user that needed guidance, I did not appreciate the future significance of those footnotes.

Now this practice is quite common in the federal government. When petroleum and natural gas were plentiful and cheap (priced artificially low by federal regulation), no one cared. But the "energy crisis," triggered by the embargo and OPEC's quadrupling of prices, resulted in a clamor within and without government. The administration came in for heavy criticism for not having an independent audit to corroborate those statistics supplied by industry.

One federal agency, however, had been quietly investigating the accuracy of natural gas reserve reporting back in 1970. The Federal Trade Commission, on behalf of the now defunct Federal Power Commission (it was one of the entities abolished when the Department of Energy was created), examined the reporting of American Gas Association new gas reserves from offshore South Louisiana. The FTC determined that AGA's reporting procedures and system could not possibly yield accurate or consistent data. In 1976, when everyone, including the Congress, had their energy consciousness raised, hearings were held in which those FTC findings were central. The congressional hearings revealed what everyone suspected: there was no government audit mechanism by which the accuracy of the industry figures could be verified.

Oil and gas reserves play a significant role in the pricing formula of the oil and gas industry. The industry, quite naturally, has a vested interest in underestimating reserves, to prepare the public for rising prices owing to a presumed energy "shortage." The industry estimates could not be duplicated or validated by government. Furthermore, the government claimed that the industry did not supply enough back-up detail for analysis.

When the Department of Energy was created in October 1977, it established a division called the Energy Information Administration. One of EIA's principal responsibilities is to collect and analyze energy information. Armed with new forms for industry to fill out and methods of statistical analysis of energy data, EIA has issued three cautiously upbeat annual reports. In addition, EIA issues a periodical called *Monthly Energy Review*, sold by SuDocs and a depository item. From reading their annual reports and glancing at a few recent issues of the periodical, I get the impression that EIA is placing a great deal of hope on something called Form EIA-23, "Annual Survey of Domestic Oil and Gas Reserves." This form is to be filled out by selected oil and gas well operators. In addition, EIA purports to have some new statistical weapons in its armory plus some that it inherited from predecessor agencies like the Federal Power Commission.

One of these weapons purporting to give EIA some forecasting accuracy is an econometric model based on the assumption that the price of oil is *the* major factor in determining the available supply of petroleum. A range of production estimates is then made under varying assumptions on price, using different price analyses for determining the production ranges of OPEC, foreign non-OPEC (like Mexico and the North Sea) and the United States. But experts outside government have testified in hearings that this EIA model is of limited value because it gives little consideration to the conservation objectives of governments, the geological fact of limited oil in the world, political upheavals (such as Iran) and economic chaos which could lower production. The EIA model, according to its critics, tends to overestimate the likelihood and size of oil production increases; and this overestimation could have serious consequences blunting the urgency to develop alternative energy sources and the need for conservation efforts.

Beyond the confusing and contradictory messages of the industry, the academicians, and the government lies another problem. The very effort to develop the best mechanism possible to monitor the suspicious reporting practices of the powerful oil and gas industry creates a dilemma. In order to do this effectively, government must enlarge its bureaucracy, hire more consultants, create more paperwork, issue more regulations—and this activity itself is costly and adds to the rate of inflation. Moreover, this is philosophically anathema to President Reagan, who campaigned successfully to "get the government off our backs." Yet, virtually every study made over the last decade concluded that oil and gas reporting by the industry has been less than ingenuous.

The most famous and probably the greatest Chief Justice of the Supreme Court, John Marshall, recognized over 170 years ago, that the federal government, which is supposed to operate on behalf of all the people, becomes seriously compromised when private corporations or other entities do the government's work. He warned that "a corporation should not share in the civil government" of the country. The "revolving door" policy, whereby high-ranking officials depart government service to sit on the Boards of Directors of corporations or as consultants to the very agencies they once ran, is a pervasive fact of life today, and in the opinion of many has caused damage to the integrity of government. The practice has, in no small measure, resulted in the tacit complicity of energy information.

An article on the Op-Ed page of *The New York Times* recently carried a whimsical aphorism that says: "You may get the Government off the backs of the people, but they will soon demand to be remounted." It may be a wiser course of conduct, despite the extra expense, to keep the government on the backs of the oil and gas industry inasmuch as our standard of living if not our very survival obliges our elected and appointed representatives to have the most reliable information possible in a world of diminishing resources. For these times and into the foreseeable future, facts and figures on our vital petroleum resources that masquerade as government information are inimical to the public interest.

Concluding Remarks

The information that we find in government publications comes from a variety of sources. Statistics that are produced by trade associations, commercial enterprises, and corporations reflect an attempt to persuade the user in support of policies favorable to the organization's competitive position. Thus organizations outside government are inclined to select for publication the data which support the position they advocate.

Information obtained by government from non-federal sources procured through contracts and grants—especially those classified as "research' '—are seldom subject to review because the granting agency lacks the talent and personnel to evaluate the qualifications of bidders and academicians skilled at writing proposals.

Information generated by government agencies themselves tends to reflect a self-serving motivation to survive and to build an empire. A perennial practice of the Department of Defense is to exaggerate the capability of our real and potential enemies and to understate our own capabilities. In cases like this, outright fabrication of data is widespread and achieved by a variety of subtle techniques.

This is not to say that all information found between the covers of a government document is fatally flawed. It is to say that we are never sure that the information we may use achieves a comfortable degree of reliability. There is an aphorism attributed to Disraeli that we ought to keep in mind: "There are three kinds of lies: lies, damned lies, and statistics."

Several years ago, Congress wanted to insure that the big oil companies did not monopolize crude oil supplies. So it set aside crude, at low prices, for small refineries. That legislation produced a boom in small, *inefficient* refineries and a *shortage* of refinery capacity for unleaded gasoline required by late-model cars. This has been dubbed an example of the Law of Unanticipated Consequences. Just as the Law of Unanticipated Consequences worked its mischief in this instance, so too the users of government information—governments themselves, industry, schools, associations—must be aware of the "unanticipated" consequences of employing information that may lead to false inferences.

One way to temper if not wholly avoid the Law of Unanticipated Consequences is to read carefullly the source notes, footnotes, and explanatory material that generally accompany the information contained in a government publication. After all, before you sign your name to an expensive insurance policy, a lease for an apartment, or any legal contract, you are advised to "read the small print."

Another way to guard against the uninformed reliance upon government information is to be especially skeptical of accounts that are filtered through the often smudged and cloudy prism of the news media. Studies have shown that even an august newspaper like *The New York Times* is inaccurate in about one out of every four stories it reports. Moreover, the constraints of time and space that characterize the electronic media exacerbate the problem of reporting complex issues or sophisticated statistical data accurately. The specter of distortion, like a menacing apparition, hovers above your television set.

The librarian's responsibility in seeing that government information is acquired, bibliographically tamed, and made accessible is well established. But is there a greater professional role in identifying problems of interpretation, of pointing out pitfalls, of warning about the unreliability of statistical data? I have no clear or final answers, and this article is simply an attempt to raise the question for further discussion. We know, however, that the library community has given a great deal of thought to the problems of interpretation and reference assistance in legal and medical information.

Many studies—some good, others not so good—have been carried out on patron use of indexes, the card catalog, and the like. But these "user studies" have addressed the issue of *document* retrieval. Fewer studies have assayed the more difficult task, that of *information* retrieval and its uses; and those that have been conducted generally relate to the use that scientists and engineers make of their periodical literature.

In an academic library, student use presumably is monitored and criticized by faculty, while professors are presumed to possess the knowledge necessary to identify the fickle, slippery data of their disciplines—although this is by no means axiomatic. But in public libraries throughout the land there are legions of Mr. FT-410s using government information. I wonder how many of them utilize this information wisely and well?

Selected Bibliography

Inciardi, James A. "The Uniform Crime Reports: Some Consideration on their Shortcomings and Utility," *Review of Public Data Use*, 6 (November 1978): 3-16.

Levine, James P. "The Potential for Crime Overreporting in Criminal Victimization Surveys," *Criminology*, 14 (November 1976): 307-330.

Mitchell, Daniel J. B. "Does the CPI Exaggerate or Understate Inflation?," *Monthly Labor Review*, 103 (May 1980): 31-33.

"A Plan for Collecting Oil and Natural Gas Reserves Data," *Statistical Reporter*, 77 (March 1977): 190-196.

Shiskin, Julius. "Employment and Unemployment: The Doughnut or the Hole," *Monthly Labor Review*, 99 (February 1976): 3-10.

Skogan, Wesley G. "Measurement Problems in Official and Survey Crime Rates," *Journal of Criminal Justice*, 3 (Spring 1975): 17-31.

U.S. Bureau of Labor Statistics. *The Consumer Price Index: Concepts and Content Over the Years*. BLS Report 517 rev. ed. (Washington: Bureau of Labor Statistics, 1978).

U.S. Congress. House. Permanent Select Committee on Intelligence. Subcommittee on Oversight. *Intelligence on the World Energy Future*. Committee Print (Washington: Government Printing Office, 1979).

U.S. Congress. Senate. Committee on Interior and Insular Affairs. *The Energy Information Act*. Hearings, 94th Cong., 2d Sess., March 9, 12 and April 2, 1976 (Washington: Government Printing Office, 1977).

U.S. President's Commission on Federal Statistics. *Report of the President's Commission*. Volumes I and II (Washington: Government Printing Office, 1971).

THE UNITED STATES GOVERNMENT PRINTING OFFICE IN THE 1980S

By William J. Barrett

When asked to speak about my vision of the Government Printing Office (GPO) in the 1980s, I immediately became leery, because every time that I am asked about the future, I flee to the words of Mark Twain: "I was gratified to be able to answer promptly, and I did. I said I didn't know." It would probably be sheer folly to venture a guess as to what the next decade will bring to the GPO, or for that matter to the library world. However, that does not discourage me from trying. But, before looking into the future, let me briefly tell you about what we do at the GPO, where we are coming from, and what our workload is like.

The Office of the Superintendent of Documents, an integral part of the GPO, was created through the passage of the Government Printing Act on January 12, 1895. The act invested in the Superintendent the responsibility for the sale and distribution of U.S. Government publications to the public and the free distribution of documents to depository libraries. By law, the Office of the Superintendent of Documents has four major responsibilities:

(1) sale of government publications,
(2) distribution of government publications to depository libraries,
(3) mailing of publications for members of Congress and the Federal agencies, and

(4) compilation of catalogs and indexes of government publications.

The following factual information suggests the diverse activities and workload of the Office of the Superintendent of Documents. It also provides insights into how the four major responsibilities are met. Now for the factual information:

> The typical government publication ranges in price from $1.00 to $10.00, although there is one subscription for all House and Senate hearings; it sells for $6700 per session of Congress.

> Approximately 450,000 letters of inquiry are received annually.

> Some 9,700 mail orders are processed daily.

> Some 25,000 different titles are kept in stock at all times.

> The 27 GPO bookstores served about 500,000 customers last year.

> About 85 percent of the business comes from mail orders.

> Mailing lists contain the names of 2,108,340 subscribers.

> A sales inventory of 34,366,195 copies of government publications is maintained.

> In 1895, 50 people were employed resulting in annual sales of $899, whereas in 1979 a little more than 1,000 employees were engaged in sales volumes of $48 million dollars.

> Two major improvements in recent years have restored our promi-nence in the mail order business to a rating of "among the top five" by a leading New York mail order consultant. They are the development of an accurate automated reference file for the products sold and an automated inventory system which provides accurate information on the location and quantities of bulk stock.

> In fiscal year 1978, Congress enacted Public Law 94-95, which removed almost all funds for salaries used to operate the sales program. Without getting too technical, a relatively small change in language forced the sales program into a pay as you go situation, the same as any private retailer. In fact, it was a bit worse, because the change did not permit us to keep retained earnings to offset possible future losses. The expenses this year may total approximately $49.5 million and the revenue may

reach about $50 million. If this projection is correct, there may be a one percent profit on sales; any profit would be returned to the treasury.

In May 1981, some 3,000 government publications were exhibited in six cities in China in the largest book exhibit ever held in the world. The Chinese Premier opened the exhibit. Great increases in sales are expected from this exhibit.

Free Distribution

The free distribution of government publications is accomplished in two ways: through the distribution facility at Pueblo, Colorado, and the Library and Statutory Distribution Service in Alexandria, Virginia. The Pueblo facility, which opened on October 16, 1971, was originally set up to distribute orders from the *Selected List of U.S. Government Publications* to those customers west of the Mississippi River. Business increased dramatically when the GPO assumed responsibility for distribution of consumer information publications which had been distributed by the General Services Administration from the Washington Navy Yard.

In March 1978, the GPO brought in a commercial consultant who specialized in mail order distribution and who assisted us in modernizing the Pueblo facility to the point where it may be the finest, most efficient, cost effective distribution facility anywhere. In fiscal year 1980, the Pueblo facility collected $4,102,230 for *Selected List* orders and the few paid publications listed in the *Consumer Information Catalog*. More importantly, approximately 30.1 million free publications were mailed from Pueblo, where there are only 84 permanent employees. The benefits realized from the modernization efforts in Pueblo include:
(1) an overnight productivity increase of 30 percent,
(2) an annual cost avoidance of over $100,000,
(3) reduction of temporary employees of 82 percent, with a resultant salary savings of $140,000 annually, and
(4) reduction of warehouse processing time of 54 percent.

Reimbursable Mailings for Congress and the Federal Agencies

Congress gives the GPO an appropriation for the work done for it, and the Federal agencies are charged on a reimbursable basis. This work is done at the facility in Alexandria, Virginia. While not yet as efficient as the Pueblo operation, the GPO is now installing the same automated corral system in Alexandria that increased productivity so dramatically in Pueblo. The GPO is requesting considerably more space for the Alexandria operation and during fiscal year 1982 expects to have in operation two automated systems: (1) a system to provide more accurate inventories, faster service to the order fulfillment and transit areas, and management reporting capabilities; and (2) a system to yield the marketing and detailed billing data required by some Federal agencies.

Depository Library Program

The depository library program is enormously popular with the Congress, but too often it is overlooked by the issuing agencies. The Office of the Superintendent of Documents administers, for the Congress, the physical receipt, storage, issuance, indexing and cataloging of all government publications to the 1,341 depository libraries throughout the country. All of these libraries were designated as depositories by members of Congress or by special law. Increased acquisition efforts, and the advent of the micropublishing program over the last three years, have had a major influence on the depository distribution program. In fiscal year 1981, distribution is expected to reach nearly 81,000 titles, with about half shipped in film format and half in hardcover. Stated another way, in fiscal year 1981, SUDOC expects to distribute 31 million copies of government publications to the depository libraries. Beginning with this, the 97th Congress, depository libraries may elect to receive all congressional committee hearings and committee prints in either hard copy or microfiche.

In brief, you may be surprised to learn that in 1979, for all the programs discussed, the Superintendent of Documents distributed 135,818,532 government publications, free or paid, to recipients in every corner of the globe.

The 1980s

I feel like the little girl that Adlai Stevenson described. She knew how to spell "banana" all right, but she did not know when to stop. However, my problem is in where to begin!

In order to explore intelligently the transition of documents into the 1980s, the progress of the previous decade must be reviewed. Before sharing a few high points of the 1970s and before exploring the possibilities of the 1980s, we need to walk back a few centuries and examine the transitions made in printing, since that is how most library material emanates. The invention of movable type in the middle of the 15th century has been acclaimed by scholars and historians as the workhorse that pulled Western civilization from the Dark Ages into the Age of Enlightenment, spreading the seeds of the Renaissance and the revolutionary change in culture, literature, politics, religion, science, industry, and technology. Printing provided a means of communication that sparked an unprecedented explosion of knowledge, discovery, commerce, industry, and human mobility.

A century after Gutenberg's death in 1468, the world was fairly accurately charted as exploration and colonization of the New World were well underway. A printing industry was flourishing throughout the Western World, especially in Italy, France, Germany, and England, where books of all sizes and contents were being published at a rate that would have astounded Johannes Gutenberg. If Gutenberg had been around one hundred years after his invention, he would have been delighted with the innovations in typography and publishing by such men as Nicholas Jensen, William Morris, Bruce Rogers, and Aldo Manutius. He would also have been amazed at the proliferation of type sizes.

Gutenberg would have been at home in any printshop in Europe, although he might have been enraged by the deterioration of artistic beauty and technical excellence of publications at that time. If he had been around in 1640, in Cambridge, Massachusetts, he would have been comfortable in Stephen Day's printshop, where the first colonial books were published. If he were around today, Gutenberg would be at home at the U.S. Government Printing Office, even though he would be petrified by the sight and sounds of modern technology. He might not even recognize it as a printing plant at the end of the 1980s. As is evident from this brief historical discussion, printing technology changed very little from 1450 to 1950, a period that spawned spectacular and incredible changes otherwise.

Developments are now occurring so rapidly that I wonder if library patrons will use hard copy in the late 1980s. Just as the invention of movable type more than 500 years ago was instrumental in spreading the world of discovery and enlightenment, the advent of the computer and automated editing and composition systems puts us today on the threshold of cybernetics information systems. Electronics newspapers, read on a TV screen and received as printed copy by the reader in his home, are being demonstrated in Japan and Great Britain. Since the phototypesetter was produced in 1946, and second generation equipment was introduced in 1963, technological developments have been rapid. A brief examination of some more recent developments in government publishing and the resulting fall out of the impact on the library community might be in order.

The 1970s witnessed the first use of optical character readers in GPO printing plants; ink-jet printing was introduced; display terminal editing systems were installed; images of halftones on a cathode ray tube photocomposer became a reality; and laser platemaking was commonplace. During the same decade, the depository library program grew from 1,031 to 1,330 libraries. The GPO began promoting government documents through the news media and at displays and conventions. The best selling publication was *Infant Care* and NASA's beautiful space publications were proving popular, especially those depicting the first lunar landings. Question-and-answer type publications on drugs (LSD, marijuana, angel dust, "uppers and downers") collectively sold more than four million copies in 1970 and perhaps reflect a commentary of the times.

Significantly, the number of entries listed in the *Monthly Catalog of United States Government Publications* each year exceeded the previous year. For the first time, in 1970, GPO bookstores sales exceeded $2 million, up from the previous year by 55 percent. That same year the GPO moved its sales stock into a 300,000 foot warehouse in Laurel, Maryland. Work was also begun on the 1961-65 *Cumulative Index to the Monthly Catalog*. The convergence of technology with word processors and electronic and plateless printing resulted in shortened production and distribution time and provided better and quicker service to the American public.

Also in the 1970s, *Monthly Catalog* and depository record automation plans were completed. Discussions were held with OCLC on implementation of *Monthly Catalog* automation plans. Cooperation with the Library of Congress was greatly expanded in the cataloging area. The name authority project was expanded to include more names. In 1979, exactly 19,580,302 publications were distributed to depository libraries—a rise of 5 million over the previous year.

With the 1980s, speculation about our professions, yours and mine, involves certain risks. Technology is easy to predict. But, it is far more difficult to predict the social reaction to technology and the reorganization of our lives around future information products. I want to take you quickly through technologies that are changing because they have already started impacting our profession.

Certainly the most dramatic and profound technology change that continues is that associated with the computer. The price-performance ratio of a computer has improved rapidly over the last few years. If television sets had improved at the same rate, they would cost eighteen cents today. The first Mark-I computer, built 25 years ago, moved a piece of information form one pole to another by sending 220 volts over a copper bus. The same function is now performed by shifting an electron from the valence of one molecule to another. Where are we headed? Experts like Christopher Burns say with certainty that computers will go the way of the steam engine, and will disappear from our daily lives. They will become so small and so inexpensive that we will use them redundantly and in general modes. Initially, computers will disappear into typewriters, producing from eight to twelve type fonts in four to six sizes, using a laser image device and be able to store all the correspondence it can produce in a year. The computer will also disappear into the home; the

Atari is only one example of what is being sold in the consumer market.

The computer will interface in the 1980s with another amazing technology, micrographics. Computer-aided retrival (CAR) capitalizes on the strong points of the two technologies; the ability in micrographics to store images on microforms at a very low cost, and the ability in computing to have machines making logical decisions under programed control.

Another area of computer technology that librarians should know about is the use of a videodisc as a random retrieval programed instruction tool. Robert Whooley, a librarian at Utah State University and his associate, Dr. Kent Wood, have done considerable pioneering on the library application of videodisc, which contains two to three hours of programing or 53,000 pages on each side. If the average book has 250 pages, three hundred such books could be stored on a single side of a silver luster 12-inch videodisc. The videodisc looks very much like the 12-inch stereophonic records played on a phonograph. The videodisc itself is a pressed "floppy" product of clear mylar-type plastic overlapping an imbedded metallic center. To repeat, almost 300 books can be retrieved and projected on a video screen from one of the discs. As an alternative up to 50 hours of high fidelity music can be stored and retrieved. Incidentally, several educational films can be stored and retrieved. What is the library application? Consider that a classic book can be recorded on a single videodisc in both the original form and in a movie version. The first one minute of storage space on the disc can be the book; a one-hour and 59 minute film of the same book can be recorded on the remaining storage surface. Students or other library patrons can read the book page by page in a single-frame sequence. Then, at their command, the motion picture sequences unfold. Videodisc can move from print to non-print at the flip of a switch. One of its great advantages is the low cost of materials. The projected materials cost of a single videodisc is approximately 50 cents; the total cost for a 30 to 45 minute videodisc program is $10.00. Thus, the cost of materials is only 5 percent of the total disc price. However, it should be noted that people cannot write yellow notes in the margin and cannot read videodisc in bed! Still, it could well be a real home appliance, designed with a microprocessor in place for education and entertainment.

Computers will also disappear into the thermostat in the 1980s. Texas Instruments has a device that will monitor the temperature and humidity of a house and control the furnace when nobody is home. The device also monitors the safety and security of the home and, if the situation demands, will automatically call the police or fire department.

Computers are not the only technology undergoing rapid change. Fibre optics make it possible to carry 5,000 high speed data lines over a piece of glass no larger in diameter than a human hair. There are several reasons why fibre optics will become a real part of the future, one of which is that it is expensive to mine copper while fibre optics are made from sand.

Several clever laboratories have connected the telephone, the television set, and a computer into a system called variously videotext and viewdata. What you can have is a telephone dialing a computer over telephone lines and connecting the data base at a central computer with a display screen, or several display screens, in the home. It has several possibilities: delivery of the news or performing as a tutor and providing individually programed instruction. This technology could well be the tool that can deliver "how to" publishing to the home or library in a way that no book has been able to do in the past. It conceivably can do your shopping while you remain home, book your airline tickets, and participate for you in the banking market, real estate market, the used car market, or the classified advertising market.

Certainly one of the most interesting technologies that has affected us, and will continue to do so throughout the decade, is the dawning of satellite communications technology. This is not new; twenty years ago President Dwight D. Eisenhower's Christmas message was transmitted by satellite around the United States. Direct-to-home satellite broadcasting is the only economic delivery system available to deliver projection holography, which is a three-dimensional television system.

The fundamental fact of any projection is that American society is getting older. The baby boom is over. Patrons who want information are growing older, and they want certain types of information. For example, they buy or borrow "how-to-do-it" books, want some novels, prefer more magazines, and read more newspapers. Adult education and continuing education will be big in the 1980s, but more of it will be in the form of videodiscs or interactive data bases. Futurists tell us that in the coming society, people will not go to the movies very much. That is why movie houses are now being built in shopping centers where they can be quickly torn apart and used later as stores. That does not mean you should not bet on the movie business if you are so inclined; it only means that movies will be delivered another way, and, most probably, more faithfully. People will have information appliances in their homes partly because their businesses will pay for them. The trend toward continuing education and exploration of personal potential means that more people will look up their horoscopes, that they will learn to speak foreign languages, and they will decide at age 60 to grow roses. Whenever they do these things, they are going to buy or borrow information.

Now, I am not assuming the role of prophet of doom for publishers and libraries. Information in the home-of-the-future will not replace the library down the street. But, it may be a different kind of product that libraries will be dispensing. Technology is changing. OCLC's Channel 2000 project was recently market tested in 200 homes in Columbus, Ohio. This home information service provides financial services such as bill paying, accesses the *Academic American Encyclopedia*, and provides home access to the computerized catalogs of the Public Library of Columbus and the Franklin County Library System, as well as that of Denison University. The system uses an ordinary television set, a telephone, and an adapter designed by OCLC, Inc. This is the first interactive home banking service to be tested in the United States, and the first multi-volume general encyclopedia to be made available via computer to remote terminals. With such a system, subscribers could, for example, pay bills or check the status of their bank account on their own television set. They could also look up an article in the *Academic American Encyclopedia* from their living room. Sons or daughters could work on their college assignment by accessing the college library from a television set in their home or in the lobby of their dormitory. Channel 2000 will also access a data base known as Comptility, which will provide information on government meetings, various views on current legislation, and extracts from Ohio laws.

Most people think they know what a library is. Perhaps they do. But I wonder how long that will be true? Libraries are going to become information clearinghouses. The variety of information services that libraries provide to citizens at home or in the library will expand. Information technology is going forward at incredible speed. With the introduction of lasers into library and printing technology, one might say it is careening at the speed of light. New technology offers the tantalizing prospect that libraries will be able to provide more information to more people in more ways. It can make each library the undisputed information source-of-choice in its community. Libraries could break their physical bonds and move right into our living room, office, or dormitory with an array of services limited only by the imagination.

Plans at the GPO for the 1980s include many mechanical enhancements to boost productivity. Of notable interest to librarians are recent improvements in the *Monthly Catalog* by adding a keyword index, and by eliminating duplication in the indexes. The GPO intends to bring about full implementation of *Monthly Catalog* depository records automation. The Library of Congress now accepts GPO cataloging as the authority for government documents. Basic requirements are also being developed for cataloging to improve the quality and timeliness of services offered through the cataloging and indexing program.

We at the GPO are thinking about a microfiche cumulative monthly index to the *Monthly Catalog*. This could even be the basis for regular 10-year cumulative fiche indexes. The age of microforms will continue, with perhaps the *Monthly Catalog* on microfiche and accompanied by on-line access via OCLC. The on-line access is already underway and may well be ready by 1984. It is now technologically possible that in each state one or both regional depository could receive suitable software so that print-out transmission of documents bounced off a communications satellite by GPO could provide quick distribution throughout the state.

The continuing trends will entail further implementation of new technology, the quest for better quality production and distribution, along with even greater satisfaction for librarians, patrons, and purchasers of government documents. An overriding theme of the 1980s will be getting the most for every tax dollar spent during what looks to be a decade of inflation and what Christopher Burns calls a decade of dislocation. He calls it that because the dislocators are of such magnitude that, at their worst, they possess the potential to disrupt our kind of service, yours and mine, and, at the very least, cause substantial dislocation in our normal patterns. These dislocators are:

Petrochemicals: How much will be available? In what form? At what price? At what cost in dollars to printing and distribution?

Distribution: Will there be alternative methods of delivery? Distributed printing—producing the product near the consumer—how close to reality? How costly?

Paper: When, if ever again, will supply catch or match demand? What will environmental controls, waste, and conservation do to paper mills?

Electronics: Electronic journalism—will it supplant or supplement books, magazines, and newspapers?

The final, and perhaps the most serious, dislocator to the future of library science is the phenomena known as "budget whittling," with attendant contributors such as revenue sharing or lack of it, inflation, Proposition-13's, and in Massachusetts Proposition 2½. Since all of these factors drastically limit the buying power of libraries, librarians need to call on their creative talent. For example, why should not public libraries make space for a small shop selling new books, government and commercial, in specialized fields, along with quality newspapers and magazines? If the modern library's function is the dissemination of information, does it matter how the function is performed? If libraries purchase such material for resale, they would get a discount ranging from 20 to 40 percent and they could add a small handling charge to the cost of the material. Moreover, the profits could be used not only for operating costs but to pay salaries as well. This is no small matter at a time when library acquisitions have been scathed by double digit inflation and budget cuts. In this connection, I should mention a decision by Minneapolis U.S. District Court Judge Earl Larson. He ruled that a library board cannot ban business activities on public library property. This could be extremely controversial. But, this is an idea worth considering because it could be good for one of the greatest institutions in the world—the endangered public libraries.

It has not been my purpose to drag anyone kicking and screaming into the 1980s; your life is not at stake; your livelihood, however, might be changing! Like it or not, the world of science and technology has become inseparable from the world of communications. This information can be either terrifying or terrific. The choice is ours. On the bright side, there is enormous potential for new ideas for a library based on the technological innovations. Remember what commercial technology did for certain people in the fine arts? Roy Lichtenstein made it big with Ben Day dots; Andy Warhol legitimized silkscreen and photo-screening as "fine art" techniques; Dan Flavin made a name for himself arranging fluorescent lightbulbs; sculptors have become welders; and art is coming out of computers.

So much for motivation. The fact of the matter is that there is no choice. Anyone involved in library science in the 1980s will have to keep up with rapidly changing technology. But while Mr. Gutenberg, in his time, and the inventors of lasers and electronics set a blistering pace in our time, keep one thing in mind: The medium does not deliver the message, communicators do. And, believe me, librarians are communicators of the first rank. Some librarians are better than others. Every age has had its specialists. When smoke signals were the medium, there were surely some Indians a little more nimble with their blankets. In the primitive African jungles, some drummers had a better beat. In the medieval cloisters, almost any Brother Dominic could grind the pigment, but only one or two penned the manuscripts. The technology of the 1980s will be mind boggling. But all of it is completely mindless and powerless without the intelligence, talent, wit, imagination, esthetic sensibility, creativity and all those other sublime qualities that only human beings possess.

Perhaps a key issue relating to information on the national level in the 1980s is treating the information that is collected, maintained, and disseminated in reports, forms, manual records, files, computer records, publications, and other information media, as a resource and managing it as a resource. The task is one that falls to the private sector as well as the government—to manage information in order to: (1) avoid duplication; (2) gain an idea of the use, value, and cost of information; and (3) standardize data across information systems. Management of information resources does not have anything to do with control or censorship of the data or information itself. The primary purpose of information resources management is to provide a tool such as an information resources directory, to be a compendium of information about the information resources. For example, if the information resource is a form, a report, or a computer file, the directory would contain information about that resource, not any of the actual contents. In this respect information resource data is similar to bibliographic data. The main purpose is to provide an awareness tool; a directory will serve as a means of determining whether or not a piece of information already exists, and if it does, will indicate where one can go to find out more about it. A Federal project now underway in the Office of Management and Budget that exemplifies this concept is the Federal Information Locator System project (FILS). FILS will provide a centralized locator file containing information about the data collected from private business, generally reported in response to Federal regulatory requirements. Federal agencies will input records into this central system about the information they are collecting. The locator file can then be checked for duplication of reporting in an effort to reduce the burden on private business. Also, before beginning collection of any new piece of data, agencies can query the file to determine if it is already being collected.

Another indication of the government's interest in this area was the announcement in February 1981 of the establishment of the Office of Information and Regulatory Affairs, reporting directly to David Stockman, the Director of the Office of Management and Budget. This new office will be responsible for the implementation of the programs set forth in the Paperwork Reduction Act of 1980.

The predictable turbulence of the next decade can cause crippling fear, or it can challenge our abilities to deal with it constructively. Sam Keen, a writer, recalled a true story about spending his childhood summers on the Atlantic seaboard near an inlet bay on the ocean. At the mouth of the bay great turbulence occurred when the tide came in and went out, and many swimmers drowned because they could not negotiate the currents. Fortunately for Keen, who loved to swim, a long-time resident told him how to master the turbulence. The trick, he learned, was knowing when to float and when to swim. His knowledge came from the water itself, from getting into the water and feeling its movement around him. When he felt the turbulence of the tide, he knew that it was time to float. When he felt the turbulence subside, he knew it was time to swim. There was little danger, he discovered, if he stayed in touch with the forces causing the turbulence which surrounded him. What Keen did in the bay we can do in information management. Instead of fighting the turbulence of the 1980s, we can put ourselves in touch with it and discover the forces creating it. As we do this, we can make the right decisions and negotiate the turbulence successfully.

Alvin Toffler wrote, in *Future Shock*, of the "shattering stress and disorientation that we induce in individuals by subjecting them to too much change in too short a time."[1] The result is "real sickness," a disease of change. This disease can be prevented by learning what the new technologies are and how to use them advantageously. We are all in the information business, and we must view these technologies not as threats, but as opportunities. We need to (and we will) seize them with the same enthusiasm of a newspaper reporter grabbing a telephone to call in a good story.

References

1. Alvin Toffler, *Future Shock* (New York: Random House, 1970).

COLLECTION DEVELOPMENT FOR UNITED NATIONS DOCUMENTS AND PUBLICATIONS

By Luciana Marulli-Koenig*

In times of financial retrenchment and shrinking storage space, interest in collection development and collection management activities has steadily grown. At first, the attention of researchers and practitions was devoted, as would be natural, to the overall collection. Recently, however, librarians have begun to study the particular problems of such special materials as government documents and, within that area, the documentation of international organizations. This article follows those efforts. It will briefly review the literature pertinent to developing and managing a United Nations documents collection; will outline the basic principles that guide collection development policies, and seek to apply them to United Nations materials; and will cover retention and weeding methods.

The article will concentrate on material issued by the United Nations proper. It will not cover texts published commercially dealing with the United Nations, nor will it cover the documentation of the specialized agencies, such as the United Nations Educational, Scientific and Cultural Organization (UNESCO) or the International Labour Organisation (ILO). However, many of the points made apply to the documentation of those bodies as well.

*The author is grateful to Dr. Elisabeth Nebehay, Chief, Collection Management Unit, Dag Hammarskjold Library, United Nations, for having provided the philosphy of collection development on which this article rests, as well as clarification and advice on many practical aspects of document acquisition discussed here.

The Literature

Among the most useful pieces of work to appear recently on the topic is *Guidelines for Collection Development*,[1] published by ALA in 1979, and now one of the Association's best-sellers. The result of several years of dedicated committee work, the *Guidelines* cover the formulation of collection development policies, the evaluation and review of library collections, and budget allocation. The *Guidelines* identify and define five collecting levels: comprehensive, research, study, basic, and minimal, in a decreasing order of exhaustivity.

Dealing more specifically with collection development of United Nations publications is an article by Peter Hajnal, "Collection Development: United Nations Material."[2] It is a thoughtful and detailed analysis of types and titles of materials to be included in United Nations collections at various levels of exhaustivity, and is likely to become a must for reading in this area.

A third useful work is *Collection Development in Libraries: a Treatise*,[3] which includes a paper by Peter Hernon on government publications, covering also United Nations documents.

Collection Development Policies

Short of great skill on the part of the librarian, the most useful tool for gathering and maintaining a workable United Nations documents collection is a written collection development policy. To facilitate the task of librarians who want to prepare such a policy, the committee on Collection Development and Evaluation Policies of ALA's Government Documents Round Table has collected library policies concerning government documents. The Committee's goal is to identify outstanding examples and to draft recommendations for a model policy. Four guidelines among those available to the Committee cover extensively United Nations documents and could be used as a basis for the drafting of policies suitable for one's own institution. They originate, respectively, from the libraries of Stanford University, the University of California at Irvine, the State University of New York at Buffalo, and the University of Washington Law School.

At United Nations Headquarters, the Dag Hammarskjold Library (DHL) has been developing since 1972 detailed policies covering the acquisition, retention and maintenance of its extensive documents collection. The Library is by mandate the major repository of the documentation of the organizations of the United Nations system. Although the collection development policies of the DHL are more comprehensive than other libraries are likely to require, it is worth discussing them in some detail, since the policies of other libraries may to a certain extent draw on them.

The basic DHL policy spells out the:
• functions of the library;

- nature of the library's collections and services;
- main categories of collecting;
- languages of the materials collected;
- collecting levels;
- acquisition priorites; and
- retention limits.[4]

Annexes I, II and III to the basic policy give detailed guidelines concerning the three main categories of materials collected:
- documents and publications *of* the UN system and the League of Nations;
- publications of research value *about* those bodies; and
- other materials of permanent or current interest to the work of the Organization.

Numerous sub-annexes (annex I has 16 sub-annexes so far) lay down guidelines applicable to specific parts of the collection or specific categories of publications. Thus, Annex I, Sub-Annex 1 covers the documents and publications of the International Monetary Fund (IMF), Sub-Annex 2 those of the General Agreement on Tariffs and Trade (GATT), and so on.

Three collecting levels are defined:
- Exhaustive: *all* material emanating from an organization or body is collected, regardless of the organ issuing it, its date, form or language of publication, its category of distribution or its substantive content;
- Comprehensive: only designated categories of official materials are collected in their entirety, for example, basic documents, official records, bibliographic works, substantive reports and studies;
- Selective: material is collected on an *ad hoc* basis in accordance with current and long-term requirements; usually only basic documents and reference tools are acquired.

Material issued by the United Nations proper is collected at the exhaustive level and for permanent retention. Material of the specialized agencies is collected at the comprehensive level. Material in other areas of the collection (e.g., the documentation of UN affiliated bodies) is acquired either at the comprehensive or at the selective level, depending on its usefulness to the Organization.

The following are some of the main categories of materials collected:
Official Records;
Publications included in official printing programs;
Material circulated in authorized symbol series;
Proceedings of conferences;
Annual reports on activities;
Budgets and financial statements;
Texts or compilations of basic documents bearing on constitutional or organizational aspects (such as charters, statutes, rules of procedure, etc.);

Organizational and administrative manuals;

Directories;

Papers presented for conferences, seminars, workshops, training courses, and institutes, meetings of experts and non-governmental organizations convened by the Organization as full sponsor or co-sponsor;

Studies prepared by the Secretariat, studies prepared by individual experts, and studies prepared on contract by institutions or individuals for the use of the Secretariat, a special rapporteur, or a group of experts;

Reports, studies and other material emanating from regional training centers, research centers or similar institutions established under an agreement with the Organizations and with funds wholly or partly supplied by the Organizations;

Tests and collections of treaties, conventions and other similar legal instruments;

Press releases and other public information material;

Bibliographies, catalogues, indexes, lists of documents and publications, and similar tools of a bibliographic nature.

The following categories are not acquired:

Manuscripts and collections of correspondence in the original;

Drawings;

Pictorial material, including posters;

Movies and filmstrips;

Sound recordings;

Musical scores;

Collections of newspaper clippings;

Maps, atlases, and other cartographic material (All cartographic material issued by organizations in the United Nations system is to be turned over for preservation to the Map Collection);

Computer tapes;

Forms;

Postage stamps and other philatelic material.[5]

The Dag Hammarskjold Library' policies are drafted to permit acquiring and maintaining the whole documentary output of the Organizations, in a fashion analogous to what national libraries do for the material produced in their countries.

Other libraries, even those serving the most advanced and sophisticated research institutions are not likely, on the whole, to need the same coverage and do not have the same language requirements. Nonetheless, the Dag Hammarskjold Library policies can be drawn upon very usefully when drafting policies for covering the UN documentation in one's own institution.

Collection Development Principles

The basic principle of keying a collection development policy to the *function of the library* and the study and research needs that it must serve is put forth in the ALA *Guidelines for Collection Development* for general collections. That principle applies just as well to documents collections. Librarians drafting guidelines for such collections may wish to refer to the mandate of their library. Indeed, it is desirable to introduce the policy statement with the mention of the functions of the library as legislated by its parent body and to follow that with an outline of existing collections and services.

The *use* made of the collection is a second basic consideration in collection development. In these financially stringent times, it is important to remember that even free material, as can often be obtained from international organizations, is not really free. The costs of acquiring, processing, binding, storing and servicing the material are large and are growing larger, especially so in the case of UN documents, admittedly difficult to control because of their very format. This militates in favor of getting and keeping only what has a chance of responding to user needs.

User studies can be the foundation on which policies are built: analyses of circulation records, reference queries, and citations, all can help our policy making. A number of valuable studies exist on those techniques.[6]

The *nature of the material* collected is a third basic consideration in drafting a collection policy. In the case of United Nations materials, documents and publications
- originate from numerous organs, e.g., the General Assembly and the Security Council, as well as from various programs, e.g., the sales program;
- are issued in field offices as well as at Headquarters;
- are issued in more than one language, primarily English, French, Spanish, Russian, Chinese and Arabic;
- are reproduced in a variety of ways (e.g., printing, mimeographing, microform);
- have different categories of distribution (e.g., general, limited, internal).
All of these points must be addressed in deciding the scope of a collection.

In practice, the sum of the considerations above should lead to the selection of United Nations material in specific subject areas. The selection would then be refined by considerations of format, language, and so on. In the majority of cases, what a library collects should be not so much material *by* the United Nations, as material *on* a topic, for example, international law, or the environment, whether or not it is issued by the United Nations. Thus the UN material acquired, whether physically integrated in the general collection or kept separate from it, should reflect the overall subject orientation of the library, and be collected at the relevant level of exhaustivity. For example, a library servicing an institution whose exclusive concern is international law would complement its collection with all UN materials in that area, whether printed and sold as publications, or mimeographed and distributed as documents of organs. It would not collect most of the statistical publications of the UN, for example, regardless of format or value, because most would simply be out of the scope of that library's collection.

Conversely, a library supporting advanced research studies in political science and economics would be interested in acquiring most of the documents and publications of the United Nations (including the *Official Records* of major organs, substantive publications and all supporting bibliographic and reference tools) because they document those fields, and serve as well for the study of the activities of a specific international organization.

Scope of UN Collections

Hajnal, in his article on collection development,[7] gives a detailed breakdown of titles that may be acquired by libraries collecting materials at the five levels specified in the ALA *Guidelines*:[8] comprehensive, research, study, basic and minimal. His article is a basic source for anyone assembling a United Nations documents collection. His suggestions are summarized below.

The *minimal* level is defined in the *Guidelines* as an area in which few selections are made beyond very basic works. Smaller public libraries might collect UN materials on this level; so might interested individuals, or libraries specializing in areas normally outside the field of concern of the UN. Titles collected at this level might include *Everyone's United Nation, Basic Facts about the United Nations*, the periodical *UN Chronicle*, and the *United Nations Statistical Pocketbook*.

Collections at the *basic* level are defined in the *Guidelines* as selective collections which serve to introduce and define the subject and to indicate the varieties of information available elsewhere. As Hajnal points out, larger public libraries or small college libraries might collect UN material on this level. Selections, in addition to those indicated under the minimal level, include major yearbooks and annuals such as the *Yearbook of the United Nations* and the *World Economic Survey* and materials of regional interest within the library's subject scope (for example, the *Economic Bulletin for Europe*).

Collections at the *study* level are defined in the *Guidelines* as those which support undergraduate or graduate course work, or sustained independent study of less than research intensity. This collecting level would be appropriate for university and large college libraries, for some very large public libraries, as well as for special libraries including governmental libraries and information centers. Materials selected would include, *inter alia*, in addition to the titles listed under the basic level, a generous selection of UN monographs and serials within the subject scope of the library (e.g., economic development, human rights, demography), relevant statistical yearbooks and other serials (e.g., *Handbook of International Trade and Development, Monthly Bulletin of Statistics*), specialized regional material as appropriate (e.g., *Transport and Communications Bulletin for Asia and the Pacific*), and as many as possible of the current and retrospective indexes issued by the UN as guides to its documents and publications (e.g., *Indexes to Proceedings* of major organs and *Cumulative Index to the United Nations Treaty Series*).

A collection at the *research* level is defined in the *Guidelines* as one which includes the major published source materials required for dissertations and independent research, including materials containing research reporting and new findings. This collecting level would be appropriate for large university and other research libraries, including those specializing in international relations. A collection at this level would include all UN publications and printed documents, including the *Official Records* of major UN organs and several or all generally available series of printed documents.

At the extreme end of the spectrum is a collection at the *comprehensive* level, defined in the *Guidelines* as a collection in which the library endeavors, so far as is reasonably possible, to include all significant works of recorded knowledge (publications, manuscripts, other forms) for a necessarily defined field. This level of collecting intensity is that which maintains a "special collection;" the aim, if not the achievement, is exhaustiveness. Hajnal suggests that some very large university, research and government libraries might aspire to a comprehensive collection of UN material. Such a collection would include, probably with language limitations, however, *all* printed and mimeographed materials issued by the UN in the general, limited, or provisional categories of distribution; materials outside regular distribution channels (newsletters, press releases, administrative instructions, etc.); and UN materials in microform.

Acquisition Methods

Hand in hand with the decision of *what* to acquire goes the decision of *how* to acquire. The methods for obtaining publications of the United Nations system are the usual ones of deposit, gift, and exchange.

DEPOSIT

The United Nations has set up since 1947 a world-wide system of depository libraries for UN documentation to make available to governments, scholars, and the public at large information both extensive and up-to-date about the Organization and its activities. The Dag Hammarskjold Library is responsible for co-ordinating and advising the system.

Depositories are designated by the Publications Board (the organ of the UN Secretariat responsible for the determination of the policies governing the preparation, production, distribution, and sale of documents), on the recommendation of the Director of the Library.

The conditions of deposit are spelled out in an administrative instruction on principles governing United Nations depository libraries[9] and in the *Instructions for Depository Libraries Receiving United Nations Materials*.[10]

There are two types of deposit: partial and full.

A partial depository is entitled to receive the following materials:

a) *Official Records* of the main organs of the United Nations;
b) publications that carry a sales code, regardless of the place of issue;
c) periodicals available upon subscription;
d) the *United Nations Treaty Series*.

A full depository receives, in addition to the material included in the partial deposit, all other documents and publications of the United Nations in the general distribution category, whether printed, reproduced by offset, or mimeographed. Both partial and full deposit include material in one of the official languages only. The choice of language rests with the depository library.

Despite the comprehensiveness of the deposit program, numerous groups of materials are not included in it. The *Instructions* spell out the exceptions, ranging from the publications of the International Court of Justice (ICJ), the United Nations Children's Fund (UNICEF), the United Nations Institute for Training and Research (UNITAR), and the United Nations Fund for Population Activities (UNFPA) to - very important -the documents in the distribution categories designated as "Limited" and "For Participants Only".

So, while the depository status entitles a library to receive large amounts of valuable material, depository as well as non-depository libraries may have to use additional sources to round out their holdings of United Nations documentation.

Conversely, depository libraries may elect to receive only certain series among those to which they are entitled. The selection can be made at the time of designation or at any time thereafter. Selection by subject, which involves the selection of individual documents from different series, is not allowed under the depository system. In those cases, weeding out of undesired materials should be done when the material is received.

Many tasks befall depository libraries, which are expected to place the material in the care of qualified staff, to keep it in good order and to make it accessible to the public at large - not just to the readers normally served by the parent institution. They are also expected to make the deposited items available through interlibrary loan.

A new depository system effective as of 1 January 1975 allows one free depository per country, normally the national library or other major research library in the capital city. If open to the public, the national parlimentary library also qualifies. All other depositories are required to pay a contribution proportional to the extent of deposit and the resources of the country where the library is located. The figures are: $960 for full and $600 for partial deposit in a developed country, and $300 for full and $200 for partial deposit in a developing country. Instead of paying the appropriate contribution, libraries may elect to fulfil their financial obligations as depository by providing material issued by them or by their parent body in exchange for the material received on deposit from the United Nations.

There are now about 320 depositories in about 120 countries and territories.

The contributions of libraries do not cover even the cost of shipment. For reasons of economy, the United Nations is therefore limiting the establishment of new depositories in countries where a number of them already exists. This is the case of the United States, where there are about 40 depositories.

The Dag Hammerskjold Library endeavors in several ways to assist the recipient libraries in the fulfilment of their depository functions. A liaison officer for depository libraries assures the contacts with libraries and provides advice in response to letters or calls. Guides to the organization of materials are prepared and distributed: an example is *United Nations Documentation: a Brief Guide*.[11]

Regional seminars are organized to train depository library staff in the maintenance and servicing of their UN document collection. Visits are made to depository libraries by the staff of the UN Library and of UN Information Centres to provide expert advice on matters of acquisition, control, and access, as well as to verify the observance of the conditions of deposit.

PURCHASE

The second main method of acquisition of UN material is by purchase. Libraries that are not depositories, as well as depositories wishing to expand their holdings, will find this method their best option. Purchases can be made from the UN itself, through the Organization's Sales Section, or from distributors. Both accept single orders for individual items in sales program, subscriptions to periodicals, and standing orders for recurrent titles such as the *Yearbooks*, for one or more sales categories, for one or more series of documents of organs, or for combinations of the above. What is available on standing order, the estimated annual price of each category and the conditions of payment are described in *Standing Order Service*,[12] available on request from the Sales Section (Room A-3315, New York 10017) or from distributors. The booklet outlines five different types of standing orders: over-all, subject category, title and series, mimeographed documents, and International Court of Justice publications.

Certain series available on standing order are not included in the United Nations depository library entitlement, for example the series of the International Court of Justice. Librarians should therefore compare the list of depository entitlements[13] and the standing order offerings to identify material of interest available under one plan but not under the other.

Standing order customers are entitled to receive a monthly statement of new publications in the sales program.[14] The statement has obvious uses as an alerting device. The United Nations Sales Section usually requires advance payment on individual orders. Libraries can also set up deposit accounts against which items will be charged and shipped promptly upon publication. Standing orders are invoiced quarterly or upon publication of recurrent items.

To facilitate the dissemination of its material, the United Nations has refrained from designating a single distributor but rather encourages sales through any recognized agent. Libraries can therefore place their ad hoc or standing orders for UN documents with the distributor or agent of their choice, rather than with the UN Sales Section. UNIPUB,*New York, and UNIFO,** Pleasantville, N.Y. are perhaps the commercial enterprises most active in this area.

UNIPUB has developed in the past ten years into the largest distributor of publications of international organizations. In addition to handling material of the UN, it is the exclusive national distributor of the publications of many organizations and programs of the UN system including the Food and Agriculture Organization of the United Nations (FAO), the General Agreement on Tariffs and Trade (EATT), the International Atomic Energy Agency (IAEA), the United Nations Environment Programme (UNEP), the United Nations Educational, Scientific and Cultural Organization (UNESCO), the United Nations Fund for Population Activities (UNFPA) and the World Meteorological Organization (WMO). It can also supply material of the International Labour Organisation (ILO), the Inter-Governmental Maritime Consultative Organization (IMCO), and the World

---

*The address of UNIPUB is 345 Park Avenue South, New York, New York 10010.
**The address of UNIFO Publishers, Ltd., is P.O.Box 37, Pleasantville, New York 10570

Intellectual Property Organization (WIPO). UNIFO, besides distributing materials of the United Nations and certain specialized agencies in hard copy, is aiming at becoming the leading agent for the dissemination of United Nations documents in microfiche.

Unlike the United Nations Sales Section, which requires advance payment on individual orders, agents usually bill only after the material has been delivered. This arrangement is generally preferred by libraries. Agents can also offer discounts on list prices, usually 10%.

Which vendor to select-whether the UN Sales Section, or one of the agents mentioned above, or perhaps the library's customary agent -depends on a variety of factors, including size of the order, performance of the vendor and conditions of payment. For example, a library collecting heavily materials of international organizations may consider UNIPUB the best choice as an agent. Because of that company's exclusive arrangements with FAO, IAEA, and others, the library could obtain all its international materials from that one source. If, on the other hand, only a few UN titles are collected, the library's regular dealer or agent for other types of materials may be the best choice.

EXCHANGE

A third form of acquisition is by exchange. Exchanges of United Nations documents and publications for the publications of other organizations and institutions are set up and managed by the Dag Hammarskjold Library, in accordance with a Secretariat administrative instruction.[15]

There are two main types of exchanges: complete and limited. Under the complete exchange agreement, all generally distributed documents and publications of the UN, printed or mimeographed, in the official language of choice, may be exchanged for the publications or library services of another institution. Under the limited exchange arrangement, a selected portion only of the UN documentation is exchanged in return for the recipient library's materials.

The initiative for setting up an exchange agreement may come from the UN Library or from the corresponding library. The agreement is normally concluded on the basis of balancing the monetary value of the material exchanged. Exchanges are made serial for serial, not monograph for monograph, as the latter form involves administrative costs too high to make it worthwhile.

As noted above in the section on deposit arrangements, libraries may fulfil their financial obligations as depositories by supplying to the Dag Hammarskjold Library material issued by them or their parent body in exchange for United Nations documents received on deposit. The depository libraries of Yale University and the University of California at Berkeley are among those that have set up such arrangements and supply publications of their university presses upon demand. At present about 500 exchange agreements are handled at Headquarters.

More restrictive exchange arrangements can exist between certain units of the Secretariat and other institutions working n the same area. Those exchanges are set up to obtain material helpful in the preparation of publications compiled by the exchanging unit, especially material of an official nature or difficult to obtain by other means. The Secretariat unit provides in exchange the publications it prepares. For example, the Statistical Office of the Secretariat exchanges the publications it produces for statistical materials produced by other organizations and national government agencies.

One word of caution: nowadays, when personnel costs absorb the largest part of a library's budget, exchange arrangements tend to be a rather expensive form of acquisition, because of the record keeping, correspondence and follow-up required. They should therefore be entered into quite carefully.

GIFTS

A final method of acquisition to be mentioned is by gift. Many international organizations disseminate at no cost material highlighting aspects of their activities, and the United Nations is no exception. The largest category of material distributed gratis includes public information items - fliers, posters, leaflets, newsletters, press releases, information kits, basic texts such as the *Charter*, and so on. They deal with a major event in the life of the Organization, such as a world conference on science and technology and the International Year of the Child, or with themes of continuing interest, such as human rights or disarmament. One of the most popular kits contains material useful in the preparation of "Model UN" sessions. The material is distributed on request by the Public Inquiries Unit at the United Nations Headquarters in New York, which will also fill, within limits, an occasional request for a single copy of a current document. However, the Unit does not maintain mailing lists, though it compiles short lists of material available at no cost.

The burden of obtaining the material is therefore on the librarian, who may well be advised on the occasion of an international event in which the UN is involved to contact the Public Inquiries Unit for information material on the topic. The answer will usually be positive.

Some individual units of the Secretariat also disseminate free material and, unlike the Public Inquiries Unit, can maintain mailing lists. Usually they distribute newsletters highlighting the work of the unit or reporting on major events in its field of competence. An example is the *Statistical Office Newsletter*, which carries early announcements of forthcoming publications and describes new procedures and programs undertaken by the Office; another is the series *Notes and Documents*, issued by the Centre against *Apartheid*, which documents the international struggle against *apartheid* and publishes significant studies on the topic. Several such new serials come into being every year. Since they are not disseminated through regular channels (for example, they are not included in either depository or standing order entitlements), it is difficult to become aware of them - even at Headquarters. No current comprehensive list exists nor is there a roster of units maintaining mailing lists for the dissemination of information material.

Preserving librarians may enlist the help of the Public inquiries Unit to locate offices working in their area of interest and query those offices as to the availability of free information material.

Libraries which need to build a comprehensive UN documents collection are likely to use a combination of all or several of the methods of acquisition described above. Thus, a depository library may place a standing order with a distributor to duplicate its holdings of often-used material; or ask to be added to a mailing list for material distributed free of charge; or set up exchange arrangements for material not otherwise available.

As few additional depository libraries are likely to be established in the future, a strategy in the use of the various methods of acquisition may suggest that material available for sale be bought, and free material obtained through mailing lists. Only in those cases in which the material cannot be had by other methods should an exchange arrangement be considered - a procedure that otherwise is not generally cost effective.

Selection Tools

How to select materials that fall within the scope of one's collection? A number of tools can help. The major ones include:
- sales catalogs produced by the Organization;
- bibliographies produced by the Organization;
- selection journals published commercially;
- notices in professional and technical journals.

The sales catalogs produced by the UN include the well-known *United Nations Publications in Print*.[16] Issued annually by the Sales Section at Headquarters, it lists substantive publications in print (not documents), grouped in 23 subject categories such as economic development (category II.B), social questions (category IV) and disarmament (category IX). French and Spanish versions of *United Nations Publications in Print* are also available. A good feature of the catalog is its being current. The usefulness of the list could be increased by a title index and a subject indexes.

A second sales catalog is *United Nations Publications: General Catalogue*.[17] It is a comprehensive, retrospective catalog in three languages (English, French and Spanish) issued by the United Nations Sales Office in Geneva.

The basic volume, covering material issued from 1946-1974, was published in 1975 and is updated by annual supplements. *United Nations Publications* has title and subject indexes in the three languages of the text, which enhance its value as a retrieval tool. Both *United Nations Publications in Print* and *United Nations Publications* cover only sales publications, not documents, although they refer to the availability of *Official Records* and other documents of organs on a standing order basis. Both contain lists of periodicals and of distributors of UN material. Additional catalogs covering only certain sectors of the documentation, such as *Official Records* are also listed.

In the second category of selection aids, that of bibliographies and lists produced by the Organization, the main title is *UNDOC: Current Index*.[18] *UNDOC* is issued ten times a year and consists of a comprehensive checklist with full bibliographic description of United Nations documents and publications received by the Dag Hammarskjold Library. It includes subject, author and title indexes. A list of *Official Records* received in the previous month, a list of sales publications and a list of documents republished in the *Official Records* or elsewhere are also included. UNDOC replaces *UNDEX, Series A,B* and *C*, published by the Library between 1970 and 1978.

UNDOC has multiple uses in collection management. The checklist of documents is arranged by issuing body and can be used in verifying the receipt of documents and in claiming material. It can also be used for selection in connection with the subject index. As *UNDOC* strives to cover material issued away from Headquarters, it can be used to identify this type of documentation, otherwise hard to locate. Items not for deposit are so identified in an annotation to their checklist entry.

The list of sales publications and *Official Records* found in *UNDOC* permits quick scanning and selection of the most recent production in those types of materials. The expression "most recent" must be taken with a grain of salt, however, as several months typically elapse between the publication of an item and its listing in *UNDOC*. Finally, the "List of documents republished" will prove invaluable in the weeding of the collection, as will be discussed later.

Other useful selection tools produced by the UN include *United Nations Sales Publications, 1972-1977*[19] and *Current Bibliographic Information (CBI)*.[20] Both have a main listing with full bibliographic description and a number of indexes. *CBI* does not cover UN publications but does list major publications of the specialized agencies and articles in periodicals of the UN and the specialized agencies.

In the third category of selection aids mentioned above, that of commercially published tools, the main selection tool is *International Bibliography, Information, Documentation (IBID)*.[21] It is published by UNIPUB.

Its "Bibliographic Record" lists, with full bibliographical description and annotation, the sales publications and selected unpriced materials (usually substantive reports or reference materials) produced not only by the UN family of organizations but by other international organizations as well. Excluded are working documents, press releases and internal materials. Listings are grouped by broad subject headings. A subject index, cumulated annually, is included.

The fourth category of selection aids, that of notices and listings in professional and technical journals and indexes, is the most varied. It includes a listing of United Nations and other international organizations documents in *Part B: Acquisition Guide to Significant Government Publications at All Levels* in the new two-part *Government Publications Review*.[22] The list is currently compiled by Marian Shabaan, Documents Librarian, Indiana University, Bloomington, Indiana, and by Vida Margaitis, Documents Librarian, Harvard College Library.The list concentrates on publications and documents of substantive research or reference value. Each issue contains 20 or 30 items. All topics are covered and entries are annotated.

Documents to the People,[23] the official newsletter of the Government Documents Round Table, ALA, has two columns of interest: Patricia Reeling's "News Publications" and Luciana Marulli-Koenig's "International Documents Roundup".

Of course, there is more: selected new publications in the *United Nations Chronicle*; a spattering of items appears in *PAIS*; and *Reference Services Review* is starting a column covering new government publications, including materials of international organizations of reference value.

The conclusion to be drawn is that there is a variety of selection tools for United Nations documentation. It is important to know those tools, and since they change and new ones are added, it is important to keep up with developments.

De-selection

Once the issues of what to acquire, by what methods and from whom are settled, and once the material is on the shelf, one has to consider what to keep and for how long. Systematic retention programs are an integral part of collection management, and guidelines on retention should be part of a collection development policy statement.

Decisions could be made *a priori* by type of material. For serials, specific retention schedules can be set up. Thus one may decided to keep the issues of a periodical for five or ten years after publication and discard them thereafter. Subject interest of the library and use made of the material would be, as in selection, the criteria for decision. Issues of periodicals that are cumulated periodically can be discarded when the cumulation is received. For example, the monthly issues of *UNDOC* can be discarded upon receipt of the annual cumulation.

In the case of monographs, older editions can be discarded when a new one is received, as can be texts whose content is superseded by more current material.

In the case of the large category of documents of organs, a few strategies are possible. Librarians are sometimes not aware that a substantial number of documents are republished. Documents issued in mimeographed form in connection with the session of an organ may be republished in the *Official Records* of that organ or, less often, as sales publications. An example are the reports of the First, Second and other sessional Committees of the General Assembly, which are republished in the *Annexes* to the *Official Record* of that body. Another example is that of the studies and meeting records of the International Law Commission which are republished in the *Yearbook of the International Law Commission*. When the republished text is received, the original mimeographed version can be safely discarded. Other instances of republication are mentioned in *United Nations Documentation*,[11] with suggestions for weeding.

Lists of specific documents republished and therefore weedable are contained in *UNDOC* as well as in the *Indexes to Proceedings* of the General Assembly, the Security Council, the Trusteeship Council and the Economic and Social Council.

Most libraries will also choose to discard duplicate copies of documents issued under two or more symbols. Such documents are shipped to standing order libraries in as many copies as there are symbols on the masthead. This is the case, for example, of the annual reports of subsidiary bodies of the Economic and Social Council, such as the Commission on Human Rights. The report of the Commission carries a symbol in the series of the Commission (E/CN.4/-), a symbol in the series of the Economic and Social Council (last year, E/1980/-), and the *Official Records* series number. Provided adequate cross references are made between series, duplicate copies of the report can be discarded.

Another form of weeding can take place when the library receives a microform version of the document, for example the Readex-produced microcards, of the UN-produced microfiches. The process of weeding out the hard copy of a document, and replacing it by its microform version permits economies of space but is certainly tedious and time-consuming; it demands faultless filing and maintenance of the microform collection. The operation should perhaps not be started unless competent support staff are readily available to carry it out.

Finally, weeding decisions may have to be made title by title or series by series. For example, a library receiving all the materials from the United

Nations Conference on Trade and Development (UNCTAD) may decide to keep indefinitely everything in the series of UNCTAD's Committee on Commodities, and discard completely the documents of the Committee on Shipping, either upon receipt or later. Alternatively, it may decide to keep the substantive reports of those Committees and discard all draft proposals, meetings records, agendas and so on in the two series. Again, subject interest and use made of the collection will be the guiding criteria in de-selection.

One last caveat on weeding: few libraries nowadays have the time, staff and funds for large-scale weeding projects. Efficient retention and continuous weeding programs should aim at making the operation as automatic as possible and performed on a current basis.

Conclusion

We have examined some of the major aspects of United Nations documents collection development: policies, principles, selection tools, acquisitions strategies, and weeding. The operations described should be complemented by the evaluation of the collection assembled,[24] which will feed data back to the policy formulation stage of collection development.

We have seen that nearly all that is published by the United Nations can be obtained by one method or another, in one format or another. Let us stress once again that *all* is not always needed to provide adequate service. Library resources can be supplemented through cooperative acquisition and retention programs, and interlending. There are in the United States more than 40 depository libraries and several hundreds more that receive substantial amounts of United Nations documents through standing orders or other arrangements. All of the depositories and most of the other libraries provide materials on interlibrary loan. In addition, the Dag Hammarskjold Library is ready to provide guidance or service. This impressive network should assure that nobody who needs it is left without adequate access to United Nations documents and publications.

References

1. Perkins, David L., ed. *Guidelines for Collection Development* (Chicago: American Library Association, 1979).

2. Hajnal, Peter. "Collection Development: United Nations Material," *Government Publications, Review*, 8A (1981):89-109.

3. Stueart, Robert D., and George Miller, eds. *Collection Development in Libraries: a Treatise* (Greenwich, Conn.: JAI Press, 1980).

4. United Nations. Dag Hammarskjold Library. "Policy Governing Devel-

opment of the Collections: Acquisition, Retention and Maintenance". 1972-
(Directive A/24 and Annexes). Unpublished.

5. *Ibid.* Directive A/24/Annex I, pp. 3-4.

6. For a review of applications to government documents, see Weech, Terry L.
"The Use of Government Publications: a Selected Review of the Literature,"
Government Publications Review, 5 (1978):177-184.

7. Hanjal, "Collection Development," p. 94-98.

8. *Guidelines for Collection Development"*, pp. 3-5.

9. United Nations. Secretariat. *Principles Governing Depository Libraries.* 17
November 1975 (UN doc. ST/AI/189/Add. 11/Rev.1 and Amend.1).

10. United Nations. Secretariat. *Instructions for Depository Libraries Receiving
United Nations Material.* 9 January 1981 (UN doc. ST/LIB/13/Rev.4).

11. United Nations. Secretariat. *United Nations Documentation: a Brief Guide.*
January 1981 (UN doc. ST/LIB/34/Rev.1).

12. *United Nations Publications Standing Order Service: a Guide for Librarians and
Booksellers.* 1978.

13. *Instructions for Depository Libraries*, pp. 2-4.

14. *United Nations Publications. New Publications.* New York, United Nations
Section, 1972(?)- . Monthly.

15. United Nations. Secretariat. *Principles Governing the Exchange of United Nations Documents and Publications.* 22 June 1971 (UN doc. ST/AI/189/Add.4).

16. United Nations. Sales Section. *United Nations Publications in Print: Checklist
English, 1980-81.* 1980.

17. United Nations. Sales Section. *United Nations Publications: General Catalogue.*
1975. With annual supplements.

18. *UNDOC: Current Index; United Nations Documents Index.* (New York, United
Nations, 1979-). (UN doc. ST/LIB/SER.M/-). 10 issues a year.

19. United Nations. Dag Hammarskjold Library. *United Nations Sales Publications, 1972-1977; Cumulative List with Indexes.* 1978 (UN doc. ST/LIB/SER.B/27; Sales
No.: 78.I.10).

20 *Current Bibliographic Information.* New York, United Nations, 1971-   (UN
doc. ST/LIB/SER.K/-). Monthly.

21. *International Bibliography, Information, Documentation.* (New York, UNIPUB,
1973-). Quarterly.

22. *Government Publications Review. Part B: Acquisition Guide to Significant Government Publications at All Levels*, Vol. 7B, No. 1-. (Elmsford, N.Y., Pergamon,
1980-). Quarterly.

23. *Documents to the People.* (Chicago, American Library Association, Government Documents Round Table, 1973-). Bimonthly.

24. Evaluation procedures are discussed in *Guidelines for Collection Development*,
pp. 9-19, and in Robinson, W.C. "Evaluation of the Government Documents
Collection: an Introduction and Overview," *Government Publications Review*, 8A
(1981):111-125.

UNESCO DOCUMENTS AND PUBLICATIONS AS RESEARCH MATERIAL: A PRELIMINARY REPORT*

By Peter I. Hajnal

Librarians are becoming increasingly aware of the importance of source material issued by international government organizations. Furthermore, the bibliographic complexity, as well as patterns of distribution and use, make the documents and publications of these organizations worthy of special attention.

Within the group of agencies known collectively as the United Nations system, or family, of organizations, the United Nations Educational, Scientific and Cultural Organization (Unesco) occupies an important place. It is one of fifteen functional bodies, called specialized agencies, which, together with the UN itself and two other organizations (the General Agreement on Tariffs and Trade and the International Atomic Energy Agency) comprise the UN system. The term 'specialized agency' seems appropriate when applied to organizations such as the International Telecommunication Union, the World Health Organization or the International Monetary Fund, but how 'specialized' can an agency be if its mandate embraces education, science and culture? This article provides an overview of Unesco's publishing and documentation pattern and discusses some problems of bibliographic control, access, and use. Since the information is based on research in progress, this article comprises a preliminary report.

*This article is based on a book, tentatively entitled Guide to Unesco, in preparation for Oceana Publications, Inc., Dobbs Ferry, New York.

Document or Publication?

At the outset, it would be useful to highlight the distinction between 'document' and 'publication'—a distinction that is often unclear. Many international organizations consider as 'documents' official records of meetings and other issuances governing or reflecting the activities of a main or subsidiary organ, while the term 'publications' implies material destined for a wider audience.

A recent paper compiled by Unesco's Secretariat defines Unesco publications as "everything published in printed form, under the responsibility of the Organization and. . .[including] books, periodicals, brochures, scientific maps and major documents of the General Conference published in volume form."[1] The same paper states that "Unesco documents. . .are papers issued by the Secretariat."[2] The various types of Unesco documents include: conference documents, background papers, information papers, administrative documents "issued under the aegis of the General Conference or the Executive Board of Unesco", so-called 'main series documents' "issued by the various sectors of the Secretariat," 'working series documents', etc.[3] If anything, this confuses rather than clarifies the issue of what is a document and what is a publication.

Content is no help, either, in distinguishing a document from a publication. Many items issued originally as documents are later reissued as 'publications' either for sale or for free distribution.

Although an official written Unesco definition of the two terms is lacking, there is a practical criterion used fairly widely by the Unesco Secretariat. This criterion is the presence or absence in a particular item of an International Standard Bibliographic Number (ISBN) or an International Standard Serial Number (ISSN). The presence of an ISBN or ISSN denotes a 'publication' whether or not the item in question is sold or distributed free of charge. To complicate matters further, the term 'publications' includes official publications such as the *Report of the Director-General on the Activities of the Organization*. Another indication of a document is the presence of a document code, although not all documents bear such a code.

Documents and Official Publications

The main policy-making body of Unesco, the General Conference, consists of representatives of Member States and meets every two years for several weeks. Its documents record its proceedings and decisions or are submitted in support of its work. General Conference documents include working documents, information documents, journals, programmes and budgets, commission and committee documents, etc. The *Records of the*

General Conference[4] are, perhaps, the most important official publications. They appear in several volumes and contain: resolutions and recommendations, verbatim or summary proceedings of plenary and committee or commission meetings, reports of commissions and committees, and lists and indexes.

The second major organ of Unesco is the Executive Board whose members are elected by the General Conference from among delegates appointed by Member States. The Board meets at least twice a year and is responsible for the execution of the programme set by the General Conference. Board documents include working documents, resolutions and decisions, summary records, information documents, etc.

The third main organ of Unesco is the Secretariat which is the Organization's international civil service, headed by the Director-General, Unesco's chief administrative officer. The present Director-General is Amadou-Mahtar M'Bow of Senegal. The Secretariat is currently divided into the following seven sectors: Education, Natural Sciences and their Application for Development, Social Sciences and their Applications, Culture and Communication, Co-operation for Development and External Relations, Programme Support, and General Administration. Other major Secretariat units include the Division of the General Information Programme which is responsible for the administration of UNISIST.

The principal types of Secretariat documents are: 'main documents' or surveys, bibliographies, etc; 'meeting documents' which include documents prepared for meetings or conferences as well as final reports of meetings and conferences; 'working documents' which are, as a rule, intended for limited distribution; and 'public information documents' intended to publicize Unesco's objectives and programmes.

In terms of quantity, Unesco's annual output is estimated at approximately 5,000 documents;[5] in one year, 1977, the agency issued 84,298 pages of documents, including General Conference, Executive Board, 'main series,' 'working series' and conference documents.[6]

Publications

Unesco's current publications policy is governed by resolution 6.51, adopted by the nineteenth session of the General Conference in 1976. The objectives of the Organization's publishing programme are wide-ranging:

to disseminate information [about] its aims and activities; to facilitate the exchange of information between specialists; to make known . . . the results of studies and investigations undertaken by the Organization; [and] to distribute manuscripts commissioned by the Secretariat and intended for the non-specialist public, on important topical themes connected with Unesco activities.[7]

Unesco classes its publications in several categories:
—information material, e.g., *Unesco; What It Is, What It Does, How It Works;*[8]
—specialized studies, e.g., *Manual on International Oceanographic Data Exchange;*[9]
—books on general subjects or particular topics for the general public, e.g., *The Child's Right to Education;*[10]
—reference works, e.g., the Unesco *Statistical Yearbook;*[11]
—scientific maps, e.g., *Geological World Atlas;*[12]
—specialized periodicals, e.g., *Copyright Bulletin;*[13] and
—periodicals for the general public, e.g., *Unesco Courier.*[14]
To illustrate the size of the publications output: in the 1977-78 biennium, Unesco published "377 titles, new or reprinted, in a variety of language versions, comprising 68,759 printed pages" as well as 296 issues of 12 periodicals.[15]

Besides pursuing its own publishing activities, Unesco has an expanding programme of external publishing and co-publishing. To give a few examples of works published externally or jointly by Unesco and another publisher:
—René Maheu's *La Civilisation de l'Universel*[16] was published by Laffont-Gonthier in Paris;
—*Ecology Abstracts*[17] is a periodical published by Information Retrieval, Ltd. and Information Retrieval, Inc., in London and New York, respectively, in co-operation with Unesco's Man and the Biosphere Programme;
—*Many Voices, One World*,[18] the recent MacBride Commission report on the 'new world information and communication order,' was published jointly by Unesco in Paris, Kogan Page in London, and Unipub in New York.
—*The Unesco Collection of Representative Works*,[19] the result of a long-standing programme of translating traditional classics of many cultures into major Western languages, consists of some 600 titles, published by various commercial and academic publishing houses in Europe and North America.

Although the scope of this presentation is largely confined to documents and publications, Unesco does issue material in other media:
—*art slides*. Unesco has produced a number of colour transparencies of masterpieces of world art, ranging from Russian icons to paintings from the Ajanta caves in India and from Flemish portraits to Latin American children's art;
—*photographs, films and audio-visual programmes* about various subjects illustrating Unesco's interest in education, social and natural sciences, culture and communication;
—*sound records* of various types, ranging from popular radio programmes

on cultural and educational topics to tape recordings of meetings and conferences;

—*computerized data bases*, such as the CDS/ISIS (Computerized Documentation System/Integrated Set of Information Systems) document storage and retrieval system or the DARE (Data Retrieval System for the Social and Human Sciences) data base; and

—*microfiche*—a major internal programme whose external repercussions will be discussed later in this article.

Bibliographic Control of and Access to Unesco Documents and Publications

In a recent item in the *New Yorker*, Daniel J. Boorstin, Librarian of Congress, is quoted as saying about his institution that "there are two problems for a great library: excess and access."[20] To a considerable extent the same two problems can be seen in examining the body of Unesco documents and publications. 'Excess' may well be the appropriate term to characterize the volume and range of material. To cite J.J. Cherns:

It has been said that 85% of international organisations' documents go unread. Concern is inevitably felt by the main international organisations themselves, who persistently...[reiterate] the need to cut down documentation and to improve the quality and intelligibility of the output.[21]

Reduction of excess and improvement of quality may be elusive goals or, at best, will take time. Meanwhile, adequate bibliographic control over Unesco material is essential.

Of several bibliographies, catalogues and indexes covering Unesco documents and/or publications, the following three are especially important:

—Unesco, *Publications Catalogue*. First issued for 1947, this annual sales catalogue lists, by subject, books and periodicals published by Unesco alone or as co-editions with other publishers. It also lists art and art education slides, and microform and hard-copy reproductions of out-of-print Unesco titles by commercial publishers. The catalogue covers a few 'official publications;' documents, however, are excluded.[22]

—*Bibliography of Publications Issued by Unesco or under Its Auspices; the First Twenty-Five Years: 1946 to 1971*. This major bibliography is classified by Universal Decimal Classification and lists almost 5,500 monographic works and serials produced by or with the assistance of Unesco. It covers 'official publications' but not 'documents' as the latter, to quote from the introduction, "are usually reproduced in limited quantity and are neither produced in bound form nor deliberately marketed."[23]

—*Unesco List of Documents and Publications*. Produced since 1972 by Unesco's Computerized Documentation System, this bibliography covers the

General Conference, Executive Board, conference, 'main series' and 'working series' documents; field mission reports; and Unesco publications. Issued quarterly, with annual cumulations, it also has a quinquennial cumulation covering 1972-76. *ULDP* is perhaps the best single finding aid for Unesco publications and documents issued since 1972. It provides adequate bibliographic control over both types of Unesco material. Bibliographic control over documents issued prior to 1972 is inadequate as far as users outside Unesco itself are concerned.[24]

Unesco produces other bibliographies, catalogues and indexes covering its own material, for example:

—*Unesco Literature Translations Programme; Catalogue;*[25]
—Index to *Records of the General Conference;*[26]
—*Scientific Maps and Atlases; Catalogue;*[27]
—*Index of Field Mission Reports.*[28]

In addition to bibliographic aids published by Unesco itself, other sources should also be kept in mind. Examples include:

—*United Nations Documents Index* (UNDI). Published by the UN Library, this major index, for the first thirteen years of its existence (1950-62), covered selected material of specialized agencies (including Unesco), in addition to documents of the UN itself;[29] and

—*International Bibliography, Information, Documentation* (IBID). This quarterly, current-awareness bibliography, which has been published by Unipub since March 1973, lists books, periodicals, maps, etc., issued by many international organizations, including Unesco.[30]

In summary, the bibliographic apparatus, or any of its components, does not provide complete coverage of Unesco's total output of documents and publications. The most inclusive single source is the abovementioned *Unesco List of Documents and Publications*. Readers may wish to consult Diana Cohen's study of Unesco's bibliographical services, which addresses the problem of bibliographic control.[31]

Access

Because *ULDP* covers documents as well as publications and because it is widely available to Unesco depository libraries and to others, many people are now aware of the existence of a vast body of Unesco material. This awareness has created an appetite that, up to now, Unesco has not been able to satisfy. While Unesco *publications* are easily available through a worldwide network of national distributors, major academic bookstores and other sources, the situation is much less satisfactory when it comes to *documents*. Granted, documents, as a rule, appeal to a narrower, more specialized audience than publications, but for that specialized audience many more documents would be invaluable for research and information purposes.

A number of Unesco's 350 or so depository libraries do, in fact, receive 'main series' and many General Conference, Executive Board and conference documents but few documents in other categories. There is considerable interest in the library community in obtaining and making widely available non-restricted Unesco documents. As the Unesco Library has been producing microfiche copies of Unesco documents (but not of publications) since the early 1970s, there would seem to be a basis for wider distribution in microfiche. This prompted the International Documents Task Force, Government Documents Round Table, American Library Association to adopt the following resolution:

WHEREAS, Unesco's own goals include the transfer of information, and indeed, the Universal Availability of Publications (UAP), and

WHEREAS, efficient access to the documentation of an international government organization as important as Unesco is highly significant not only to agencies of Member States but to all researchers, students and libraries and

WHEREAS, Unesco ought to serve as the model for rapid and expert dissemination of an organization's document output, and

WHEREAS, access to the materials indexed in the *Unesco List of Documents and Publications* is frequently difficult or impossible,

BE IT RESOLVED, that the Government Documents Round Table of the American Library Association and its International Documents Task Force urge that Unesco, as rapidly as possible, deposit within its designated depository libraries a complete collection of those documents available on microfiche and indexed in the *Unesco List of Documents and Publications*. The Government Documents Round Table and its International Documents Task Force also strongly recommend the establishment of an efficient sales and distribution mechanism for both the complete microfiche collection and for individual documents which libraries and individual researchers may wish to acquire.[32]

The resolution was approved by the Government Documents Round Table on June 27, 1979 and sent to the Library, Archives and Documentation Services Division of Unesco. Still, no change in the situation has occurred thus far.

Use

The use of Unesco documents and publications, like the use of any group of government documents and publications, is a very complex matter. Most librarians tend to discuss it in the light of their own experience. Such a treatment may be useful and interesting but it hardly constitutes scientific method. Theoretical analyses or quantitative studies are rare. An excellent recent work is Peter Hernon's *Use of Government Publications by Social Scientists*[33] in which he lays a quantitative foundation to his examination of the use and non-use of United States goverment publications by this important group of researchers. Similar surveys of the use of international organization documents and publications would certainly be worthwhile. Luciana Marulli expresses the need for such studies in her book, *Documentation of the United Nations System; Co-ordination in Its Bibliographic Control.*[34]

A step in the right direction is Robert Goehlert's study of the use of government documents, including Unesco material. In a citation analysis of the journal *International Organization* from 1972 to 1976, he found that of all the citations to publications of the UN system, citations to Unesco publications amounted to 20.9% of the total (116 citations out of a total of 555). This puts Unesco in the second place after the UN itself, whose publications account for 362 citations, or 65.2% of the sample.[35]

Statistical works comprise the most frequently used type of Unesco material in university and other research libraries. Graduate students, faculty, commercial firms and individual researchers need statistics collected and published by Unesco, in order to study such topics as literacy rates in a particular country, multi-country comparisons of secondary and post-secondary school enrollment, national expenditure on science and technology, or the number of television sets in various developing countries.

Legal material, such as texts of international conventions (embodied, as a rule, in General Conference resolutions), are consulted from time to time. Cultural, communication, and science policy studies, dealing with specific countries, are in some demand. Major periodicals such as the *International Social Science Journal*,[36] the *Unesco Courier*[37] or the *Copyright Bulletin*[38] are used with some frequency.

Unesco publishes many important reference works: general sources as well as directories, thesauri, bibliographies and methodological handbooks in the fields of education, natural and social sciences, culture and communication. Examples of these are *Study Abroad*,[39] *World List of Social Science Periodicals*,[40] and *Index Translationum*.[41]

An example of a topical and rather controversial Unesco publication is the report of Sean MacBride's International Commission for the Study of Communication Problems, referred to earlier in this article.[42] This report, a major source of Unesco's so-called 'New world information and communication order,' is likely to be in the news for some time, since it is about the news.

The examples just discussed support the view of Robert Schaaf of the Library of Congress that "use of international documents in libraries is primarily subject-oriented."[43]

A more specialized type of use of Unesco material can be discerned from interpretative works about Unesco and its various organizational or programme aspects. The following three examples illustrate different approaches used by authors, each of whom had a different relationship to Unesco.

James P. Sewell, an American political scientist now teaching in Canada, is a specialist in international organization and international law. His book, *Unesco and World Politics; Engaging in International Relations,*[44] is a scholarly examination of the ways and results of involvement of individuals, states, and non-governmental and intergovernmental organizations in the formation and evolution of Unesco. Sewell uses a whole battery of sources: documents and publications of Unesco and its forerunners; non-Unesco material such as monographs and essays about international organization in general and Unesco in particular; articles in a number of American and European newspapers; scholarly and popular periodicals and yearbooks; United States government publications; clipping files; proceedings of learned societies; personal interviews; letters and memoranda; unpublished doctoral dissertations; and manuscripts in Unesco Archives.

Vadim Sobakin, an international lawyer and former Soviet ambassador to Unesco, wrote a small book entitled *Unesco; Problems and Perspectives.*[45] In it, he analyzes, from an orthodox Marxist-Leninist point of view, Unesco's development, programmes, financing, personnel problems and political attitudes. To support his ideological slant, Sobakin uses, effectively but rather selectively: Unesco documents and publications; articles in Soviet and Western newspapers and periodicals; monographs about Unesco; and the British Hansard.

Richard Hoggart, a British professor of literature, was Unesco's Assistant Director-General for the first five years of the 1970s. His book, *An Idea and Its Servants; Unesco from Within;*[46] is an examination of Unesco's various organizational characteristics, constituencies, activities, but, most of all, its Secretariat. In addition to using Unesco documents and publications, Hoggart draws upon UN documents and such secondary material as monographs, periodical articles and speeches on the topic of world politics, international organization in general and the UN system and Unesco in particular. A number of items in his bibliography deal, naturally enough, with problems of the international civil service. Besides using written material, Hoggart draws heavily on his personal experience and that of his former colleagues at Unesco's Secretariat.

Concluding Remarks

This brief account has discussed certain aspects of Unesco's documents and publications: questions of kind and quantity, bibliographic control, access, and use. Other aspects merit attention as well, for instance: documents and publications of Unesco issued outside its headquarters, the question of co-ordination among the UN system of organizations, availability of computerized data bases, general problems of selection and acquisition, special problems of the Unesco depository system, and factors affecting the amount and type of use of Unesco material.

References

1. Unesco. Secretariat. "Unesco Publications and Documents," paper submitted to the Second World Symposium on International Documentation, Brussels, 20-22 June 1980 (UNITAR/AIL/SYM.2/BP.1, Corrigenda).

2. *Ibid.*

3. *Ibid.*, pp. 3-4.

4. Unesco. General Conference. *Records of the General Conference.* 1st- session; 1946- Paris.

5. Marulli, Luciana. *Documentation of the United Nations System; Coordination in Its Bibliographic Control.* (Metuchen, NJ: Scarecrow Press, 1979), p. 81.

6. Unesco. Secretariat. *Op. cit.*, p. 5.

7. Unesco. General Conference. *Records of the General Conference* (Nineteenth Session, Nairobi, 26 October to 30 November 1976. Vol.1, Resolutions), p. 62.

8. *Unesco: What It Is, What It Does, How It Works.* Paris: Unesco, 1980.

9. *Manual on International Oceanographic Data Exchange.* 3d rev. ed. Paris: Unesco, 1973. 63 p. (Intergovernmental Oceanographic Commission technical series, 9)

10. Mialaret, Gaston, ed. *The Child's Right to Education* (Paris: Unesco, 1979).

11. Unesco. *Statistical Yearbook.* 1963- Paris.

12. *Geological World Atlas*/comp. by International Geological Mapping Office for Unesco and the Commission for the Geological Map of the World. Paris: Unesco, 1976-.

13. *Copyright Bulletin; Quarterly Review.* Vol. 1- 1967- Paris: Unesco.

14. *The Unesco Courier.* 1st- year; 1948- Paris: Unesco.

15. Cherns, J.J. "Intergovernmental Organisations as Publishers: a Critical Look," paper submitted to the Second World Symposium on International Documentation, Brussels, 20-22 June 1980 (UNITAR/AIL/SYM.2/WP.I/3), p. 5.

16. Maheu, René. *La Civilisation de L'universel* (Paris: Laffont-Gonthier, 1966).

17. *Ecology Abstracts.* Vol 6- Jan. 1980- London/New York: Information Retrieval. (Continues *Applied Ecology Abstracts*; issued in co-operation with the Unesco Programme on Man and the Biosphere).

18. *Many Voices, One World; Report by the International Commission for the Study of Communication Problems*(London: Kogan Page/New York: Unipub/Paris: Unesco, 1980).

19. For a full listing see *Unesco Literature Translations Programme; Catalogue, 1978.* (Paris: Unesco).

20. "The Talk of the Town: the Librarian of Congress," *New Yorker,* (January 5, 1981), p. 24.

21. Cherns, J.J. *Official Publishing: an Overview.* (Oxford: Pergamon, 1979), p. 327.

22. Unesco. *Publications Catalogue.* 1947- Paris.

23. *Bibliography of Publications Issued by Unesco or under Its Auspices; the First Twenty-five Years: 1946 to 1971.* (Paris: Unesco, 1973).

24. *Unesco List of Documents and Publications.* 1972- Paris: Unesco.

25. See Note 19.

26. See Note 4. Indexes have appeared as volumes of the *Records* or as separate documents.

27. *Scientific Maps and Atlases; Catalogue 1976.* Paris: Unesco. (This catalogue is issued at irregular intervals.)

28. *Index of Field Mission Reports, 1947-1968.* Paris: Unesco, 1969. vii. *Index of Field Mission Reports.* 1969- Paris: Unesco.

29. *United Nations Documents Index.* Vol. 1-24; 1950-73. New York: United Nations, Dag Hammarskjold Library (ST/LIB/SER.E/-).

30. *International Bibliography, Information, Documentation.* Vol. 1- March. 1973- New York: Unipub.

31. Cohen, Diana B. "Unesco's Bibliographic Services," *International Library Review,* 9 (1977): 127-160.

32. "Resolution on Unesco Publications," *Documents to the People,* 7 (September 1979): 213.

33. Hernon, Peter. *Use of Government Publications by Social Scientists.* (Norwood, NJ: Ablex Pub. Co., 1979).

34. Marulli, Luciana. *Op. cit.,* p. 197.

35. Goehlert, Robert. "A Citation Analysis of *International Organization;* the Use of Government Documents," *Government Publications Review,* 6 (1979), 189.

36. *International Social Science Journal.* Vol. 1- 1949- Paris: Unesco.

37. See Note 14.

38. See Note 13.

39. *Study Abroad.* Vol. 1- 1948- Paris: Unesco.

40. *World List of Social Science Periodicals.* 5th, rev. ed. Paris: Unesco, 1980. 447 p. (World social science information services, 1)

41. *Index Translationum.* 1- 1948- Paris: Unesco.

42. See Note 18.

43. Schaaf, Robert. "International Documentation: Serving Users' Needs," paper submitted to the Second World Symposium on International Documentation, Brussels, 20-22 June 1980 (UNITAR/AIL/SYM.2/WP.III/2), p. 9.

44. Sewell, James P. *Unesco and World Politics; Engaging in International Relations.* (Princeton: Princeton University Press, 1975).

45. Sobakin, Vadim. *Unesco; Problems and Perspectives.* (Moscow: Novosti, 1972).

46. Hoggart, Richard. *An Idea and Its Servants; Unesco from Within.* (London: Chatto & Windus, 1978).

COLLECTION DEVELOPMENT AS REPRESENTED THROUGH THE GPO AUTOMATED LIST OF ITEM NUMBERS

by Peter Hernon
Gary R. Purcell

Dramatic increases in costs combined with moderate increases in funding have forced many libraries to examine previously held views relating to the size and growth of collections. As funds for the expansion of collections have become more limited, libraries, more than ever, must adopt carefully considered collection development policies covering all components of the library collection including the holdings of government publications. The purposes of this chapter are to comment on the application of collection development principles to goverment publications, to review the literature concerned with this, and to report initial findings of a study currently underway which uses item number data from the Government Printing Office as a reflection of library collection development practices.

The reminder of Adelaide Hasse is as true in the 1980s as when she stated it in 1906: government publications are not an inexpensive reference resource. Their "comparative limited use . . . in the majority of libraries when compared with the cost of cataloging and maintenance probably makes them one of the most expensive assets of a library."[1] Cost considerations underscore the importance of collection development.

Government publications are often separated from other library collections, and even within a documents department, there is often a separation of materials by format. For example, paper copies are usually found in one place whereas microformatted publications are generally in another location. Users must, therefore, think of government publications in the context of their information need and learn to be aware of alternative formats when they utilize these materials. Bernard M. Fry has characterized the utilization of document collections this way:

> Library administrators need to consider government publications collections [as] an information resource on an equal basis with books and serials to the extent that they are integrated in information services, whether shelved as separate collections as in many research libraries. The relationship between the documents collection and other library collections should be that of a single resource in meeting user needs. To restate: the key to a good government documents collection is integration into the mainstream of library information service."[2]

Collection Development

Collection development encompasses three activities: planning (the formulation of goals, objectives, and priorities for selection and retention), implementation of the planning policy (making documents of value to clientele accessible) and evaluation.[3] By determining the breadth and depth of collecting, libraries decide how widely to collect for a particular level of government, agency, subject, and discipline. Exhaustiveness in the provision of all available material on a topic should not be the goal, but rather the selection of what is most essential and useful to a library's clientele.

Collection development requires attention in two areas: (1) those activities within the institution, and (2) development of prompt and reliable document delivery capabilities for the exchange of materials among cooperating libraries. The second is especially important because the lack of an effective document delivery system deters libraries from limiting their document collection building to a highly selected body of materials. The lack of effective document delivery systems has undoubtedly resulted in the development of microform collections as a means of compensation for inadequate resource sharing.

The U.S. Goverment Printing Office and other distributors of official publications need to encourage the maintenance of functional collections (e.g., those resources most frequently required by the clientele) and to make recently issued publications available to depository libraries in a timely manner; otherwise, information users will continue to rely on other source providers and will be less receptive to publicity efforts for document collections.

Review of the Literature

The literature of library science is replete with statements that partial depository libraries should implement a systematic weeding program and *selectively* acquire government publications in order to avoid congestion in processing, servicing, and storage space. However, collection development, as reflected in the literature, has often been equated with selection and the acquisition process. As already noted above, collection development involves more than selection and acquisition. It is a decision-making process which is dependent upon a knowledge of user needs and patterns of use.

Studies concerned with document use by researchers indicate that documents collections are not utilized to their potential, in part because researchers find that too much time is required to identify and locate the needed government publications. Negotiating separate collections which are arranged by specialized classification systems is a time-consuming process, and the information found might be disproportionately limited compared to the amount of time expended in the search. This problem is due in part to the fact that the federal government (as well as other levels of government) publishes so extensively it can be difficult to locate the few publications most beneficial to a user's particular information need. Thus, in the case of federal depository libraries, the development of a usable documents collection depends on more than the *number* of depository categories selected.[4] It also depends on *which* categories are selected. This suggests that the application of collection development principles to the selection and maintenance of government publications collections might do much to improve the effectiveness of the choices made to improve and enhance the utilization of document collections.

There is relatively little literature available on collection development for government documents, thus the librarian interested in pursuing this at present can rely, only to a limited extent, on published information for guidance. The constant increase in the number of new depository libraries and in the number of series titles available for depository distribution underscores the urgency of research on collection development.

Only a few studies provide insights into patterns of use and can be used as a basis for developing collections. Studies of the use of monographic, periodical, and government document literature by social scientists reveal definite patterns. It would seem that a few document types and titles account for a large percentage of use.[5] However, further research needs to identify core collections of government publications for specific disciplines and to adopt the structure of literatures approach characterized by James Baughman.[6]

One author tried to identify core document titles selected by law school libraries.[7] Because the survey did not employ a structure of literatures approach, the findings did not produce recognizable, generalizable patterns. The author could only conclude that the concept of a "basic" collection was open to interpretation. In order to obtain generalizable findings, she might have viewed specific document titles and types within the context of subject specialties common to the legal field. The survey is still useful, but the lack of generalizable patterns suggest that collection development should be studied in a subject context.

Other authors have given attention to collection development, with a focus on topics such as technical report collections and their evaluation,[8] selection and retention for law school libraries,[9] development of a selection policy and the advantages of a community survey,[10] the need for a collection development policy statement,[11] and basic philosophical/conceptual issues central to documents collection development.[12] The publication which deals most centrally with varied aspects of public documents collection development and the need for a research base is a special issue of *Government Publications Review* (Volume 8, 1981, Numbers 1 and 2). This issue contains seven articles, the titles and authors of which are listed below:

(1) "An Integrated Approach to Government Publication Collection Development," by Charles R. McClure;
(2) "Collection Development for Government Map Collections," by Charles A. Seavey;
(3) "U.S. Government Publications Collection Development for Non-Depository Libraries," by Gary R. Purcell
(4) "Collection Development and State Publications," by Terry L. Weech;
(5) "Collection Development and Local Documents," by Michael O. Shannon;
(6) "Collection Development: United Nations Material," by Peter I. Hajnal; and
(7) "Evaluation of the Government Documents Collection," by William C. Robinson.

Documents librarians at present are very interested in collection development and the evaluation of their collections. Undoubtedly the reasons for this interest are: (1) more publications are available than most partial (and even some regional) depositories can absorb, (2) more libraries are operating in a zero growth situation in which space is a critical problem, and (3) typically the number of staff assigned to documents work is exceedingly small. Complicating the picture is the inability of the GPO depository program to serve, in a formal sense, as a network in which there is prompt physical delivery of needed documents to any of the requesting 1,342 depositories.

In brief, the study and practice of systematic collection development for government publications is still in the infancy stage. However, as more studies analyze selection patterns among library types, greater insights will be obtained. Related studies must focus on use patterns and match use to selection. The results of these studies should enable libraries to be better able to build functional documents collections. The design and the preliminary findings of the study reported here are concerned with the selection patterns among depository libraries as reflected in the choice of item numbers made by those libraries.

Introduction to the Study

The remainder of the chapter is a preliminary report of a study which the authors are currently conducting. For this study we have had access to the automated item number file developed by the Government Printing Office and the file of responses to the GPO's Biennial Survey, conducted in 1979. Additional data about depository libraries are currently being gathered from other sources. After presenting an historical account of how these files were acquired from the GPO, the authors will characterize the nature of the data in each of the files and indicate what can be done with these data.

History of the Study

In January 1979, while attending the ALA Midwinter meeting, the authors learned that the GPO was involved in a project to develop a machine-readable file of the item number categories received by each depository library. The purpose of the item number file is to give the GPO a better management information system for the distribution of publications through the depository system. Depository libraries select public documents from the GPO depository system by category and these categories (currently more than 4,000) are identified by unique numbers known as item numbers. In some instances the categories consist of only a single annual publication such as an annual report. In the majority of instances, however, the categories consist of a homogenous or heterogenous series of publications such as "Farmers Bulletins" or "Agriculture Handbooks".

The item number file of the GPO serves as a means of determining the categories of documents currently received by depository libraries. It is not a list which reflects choices over time, but identifies current choices at the time the file was created. It is in effect then, *a record of the current depository collection development choices*. Because of this, the existence of the file offered an unparalleled opportunity to examine government document collection development in a way not previously possible. The potential for useful insights into the depository library collection development process is further expanded with the knowledge that data acquired by the GPO from the 1979 Biennial Survey of depository libraries (also in machine-readable form) can be combined with data from the item number file.

After learning that these files were in preparation, we contacted Mr. Carl LaBarre, Superintendent of Documents, and Mr. Jim Livsey, then Director of the Library and Statutory Distribution Service of the GPO, to obtain approval to acquire and use the files. We also submitted a formal proposal in which we indicated how we expected to use the data, what we expected to obtain from them and the value which this would have for the GPO, depository libraries, and others concerned with the dissemination of government information.

The creation and authentication of the item number file required more time than anticipated by the GPO. Discrepancies between the GPO's records and those of the depository libraries had to be resolved. However, once these were resolved, the files became available for use. During this time, Mr. Jay Young replaced Mr. Livsey as Director of the Library and Statutory Distribution Service. With the approval and cooperation of Mr. LaBarre and Mr. Young, we received tape copies of the files for use in our analysis. We also received invaluable assistance from Ms. Janet Erikson of the GPO.

Description of the Files and How the Data Will Be Analyzed

Three data files were obtained from the GPO for use in this study. These are each identified below:

1. *Depository Library Directory*, which provides all depository libraries with the name, address, depository library number, and an indication of the status of the depository (e.g., whether a regional or selective depository).

2. *Item Number File*, which contains the item number categories received by each depository library at the time the file was duplicated. When acquired from the GPO, this file was arranged by item number with all depositories which received that number listed following it. This file was recoded for arrangement by depository library number; all item number choices followed the library number. This was done in order to facilitate analysis of the data.

3. *Biennial Survey*, which records responses to the 1979 Biennial Survey conducted by the GPO Library and Statutory Distribution Service. This survey consisted of 51 questions to which depository libraries were asked to respond. Some 1,286 libraries responded and the results were compiled and published in summary form in October 1979. The questions were intended to provide the GPO with information useful in the admin-

istration of the depository system. However, several of the questions have collection development significance, and when combined with other data render some interesting results. Examples of pertinent questions are:

a. Q. 15: "Approximately 4,000 items are available for depository selections. What percent has been selected by your depository?"
b. Q. 16: "Has your library reviewed its depository selections in the past two years, deleting and adding according to your community requirements?"
c. Q. 23: "Have you discarded publications retained for five years or more during the past twelve months?"
d. Q. 25: "What is the distance of the nearest designated depository from your library?"

In addition to these three files, we are in the process of constructing a fourth file which will contain further information about each depository library. This supplementary information is necessary because the Biennial Survey does not include a number of variables necessary for this study. For example, as shown in Table 8-1, we are categorizing depository libraries represented in the item number file by type. In the case of academic libraries, pertinent variables include:

Highest degree offered
Student enrollment of the institution
Faculty size
Size of collection
Publicly or privately controlled
Curriculum information for selected institutions

As for public libraries, the variables are:

Is it located in the central city, suburb, or rural area
Population of the community served.

As is evident with these additional data, smaller groups of libraries can be established within each broad type of library. For example, the item number selections of baccalaureate granting public and private institutions can be profiled in each of several size ranges.

Use of the Data

The files described above contain potentially useful information which reflects the collection development practices of depository libraries, individually and collectively. The first major step toward full utilization of this

Table 8-1: Depository Libraries by Type

Type	Frequency	Percent*
Academic	755	56.8
Public	272	20.5
Law School	175	13.2
U.S. Government	45	3.4
Special	32	2.4
State	43	3.2
Other(e.g., historical societies, the American Antiquarian Society, and the Boston Atheneum)	8	.6
	1330**	100.0

*Percentages are subject to rounding.
**The authors plan to discover why the file does not reflect all 1342 depositories.

information is to identify the general patterns of item number selection by depositories. If the item number choices made by individual libraries reflect the depository collection development practices of those libraries, then a summing or cumulation of item number selections by all depositories (or selected subsets of depositories) will show the patterns of collection development which exist among depositories. The availability of this information will enable us to characterize depository collection development by a combination of factors such as type of library, type of community, size of library, and size of community. This type of knowledge ought to be of value both to the people who administer the depository system and to the individual depository libraries.

As patterns of item number selection are identified, certain questions must be kept in mind:

1. Which specific government publications are most frequently selected by depositories? Which are most frequently selected by each type of depository?
   To respond to this question, a ranking of the most commonly acquired item number categories will be developed for *all* depositories and for various subsets. Answers to these two questions can then be obtained by consulting the ranking of item numbers by frequency of their distribution. Ranking of the item numbers is useful as a beginning because it provides a measure of the consensus as to the importance of any item number category. However, it is important to remember that this is a measure of what is rather than what ought to be in depository collection development. Nevertheless, it is a useful beginning point.
2. Which types of government publications are most frequently selected by all depositories or by each subset of depositories?
   To determine this, such categories as legislative publications, statistics and consumer publications will be established; the cumulative frequencies of item numbers in each category will then be tabulated. The purpose is to obtain a measure of the relative importance attached to those categories selected.
3. Are there differences in those types of government publications selected by depositories. Differences might be associated with the type or size of library, or size of community served.
   Some differences ought to exist because of the different constituencies served. However, until the data are analyzed, we cannot tell if those differences follow a pattern reflecting statistical significance.
4. What level of association exists between factors related to collection development and actual collection development patterns?
   For the purpose of this study, the factors related to collection development will be represented by questions which were on the Biennial Survey. Responses to these questions will then be cross tabulated with actual collection development patterns as found in the item number file. For example, what are the patterns of collection development of those libraries which answered "No" to the question "Does the depository selection provide sufficient coverage of government publications to handle the documents needs of your library users?"
5. What association appears to exist among factors related to collection development?
   One might expect, for example, to find a relationship between the number of professional or non-professional staff members available to service the documents collection and the practice of discarding gov-

ernment publications. Research should reflect if that relationship exists, and if so, how strong it is.

These then are some of the questions which we will keep in mind as we analyze the data from the files made available from the Government Printing Office and augmented by our own data collection. At the time of this report some of this analysis has already taken place. The following section reports some of the preliminary findings as a result of this analysis.

Preliminary Findings

These preliminary findings, which only represent a part of the expected analysis, have not been subjected to careful scrutiny because of limited time since the files became available for analysis. Our purpose is to illustrate what we expect to do with this data and to raise questions which require further exploration.

The following discussion will be divided into five broad categories, the first four of which will be concerned with the ranking of item numbers. The fifth will display some results of the cross tabulation of responses to questions from the Biennial Survey. The five categories of analysis are as follows:

1. All depositories-ranking of the 200 most frequently selected item numbers;
2. All depositories-ranking of the 200 least frequently selected item numbers;
3. Type of library-ranking of the 200 most frequently selected item numbers;
4. Depositories by percent of item numbers received-ranking of the most frequently selected item numbers; and
5. Cross tabulation of selected factors which are related to collection development-taken from the Biennial Survey.

Each of the five categories of analysis will be discussed, followed by a table which depicts the results of the analysis.

1. All depositories-ranking of the 200 most frequently selected item numbers.

The frequency for the 200 most commonly received item number categories has been ranked. Incidentally, the number 200 was seleced because it was large enough to provide some spread, but not so great as to create an "overload" of data at this point.

In order to display this information in a fashion which makes it comparable with other rankings, four benchmark ranking points (1, 50, 100 and 200) have been established. For each of these rankings there are two columns, one which shows the number of libraries which receive the item number represented by the rank number and the other column which indicates the percentage of the total depositories which receive that item

Table 8-2: All Depositories-Ranking of the 200 Most Frequently Selected Item Numbers

N=1330

Item Number Rank	Number Libraries Selecting	Percent Libraries Selecting
1	1281	96.3
50	1026	77.1
100	907	68.1
200	787	59.1

Table 8-3: Twenty Most Frequently Selected Item Numbers

Rank	Series Title	No. Libraries Selecting
1	Monthly Catalog	1281
2	Statistical Abstract	1274
3	U.S. Government Manual	1269
4	Congressional Directory	1255
5	Statistical Abstract Supp.	1241
6	Zip Code Directory	1207
7	Monthly Labor Review	1205
8	Dept. of State Bulletin	1192
9	U.S. Code and Supp.	1183
10	Federal Register	1166
11	L.C. Subject Headings and Supp.	1165
12	Educational Directory	1163
13	Catalog of Federal Domestic Assistance	1154
14	Public Papers of the President	1147
15	Statutues at Large	1147
16	Uniform Crime Reports	1136
17	Congressional Record	1129
18	Weekly Compilation of Presidental Papers	1119
19	Agriculture Department Yearbook	1115
20	Monthly Checklist of State Pubs.	1113

number. Thus, in Table 8-2, 1281 (the first ranked item number) represents 96.3 percent of the total number of depositories.

As previously indicated, the ranking of item numbers is a measure of the consensus which exists among libraries as to the value of the item number category. Therefore, the percentage column is the one to watch because it reflects the percentage of decline in the consensus at each benchmark ranking. The faster that drop occurs, the more quickly the consensus fades.

An examination of Table 8-2 shows that the drop seems rather precipitous. There is total consensus on none of the item number categories and by the time the ranking drops to the 50th ranked item number, barely three-fourths of the depositories select it. By the time the ranking drops to 200, the consensus has decayed to less than two-thirds. It is important to keep in mind that this is 200 item numbers out of a total of more than 4,000. Because only the first 200 were ranked, it is difficult to know the rate of decline for the entire universe of item numbers.

In addition to the ranking by frequency shown in Table 8-2, it should be of interest to know which item number categories were the most frequently selected. Table 8-3 identifies the first twenty of these by the series title assigned by the library of the Superintendent of Documents.

2. All depositories-ranking of the 200th least frequently selected item numbers.

A ranking of the 200 items least frequently selected is reported in Table 8-4. It is interesting to compare the nature of the rankings in this table to those in Table 8-2, which ranks the most frequently selected items.

Four items are received by only 1 library each; the number then jumps sharply to 32. The rate of change at this end of the spectrum is much different than at the other end. By the 200th item number ranked from the bottom, there has only been a change of 6.7 percent, which is substantially less than the percentage of change from the top. The nature of the publications is substantially different also. Discounting the first four where only a single library selected each, all but one of the next 20 series are flood control studies, by state. In fact, all but two of the next 50 ranked series are flood control studies.

Without a full ranking of all item numbers, one can only speculate as to the meaning of the data shown in tables 8-2 and 8-4. One possible meaning is that there is far less agreement in item number selection among depositories than one might suppose. It will be interesting to see if this remains true among smaller, more homogenous groupings of libraries. A second explanation is that there is a substantial number of item number categories received by very few libraries. It may be of value to know what those item numbers are and which libraries receive them.

Table 8-4: All Depositories-Ranking of the 200 Least Frequently Selected Item Numbers

N=1330

Item No. Rank From Bottom	No. Libraries Selecting	Percent Libraries Selecting
1	1	.075
50	47	3.5
100	79	5.9
200	90	6.7

Table 8-5: Percent of Libraries which Selected the 200th Ranked Item Number

Type of Library	Percent
All Libraries	59.1
Academic	65.1
Public	71.3
Law	12.0
U.S. Government	46.6
Special	46.8
State	55.8

Table 8-6: Depositories by Percent of Item Numbers Received-Ranking of the 200 Most Frequently Selected Item Numbers

Libs. by Percent Item Nos. Selected	No. of Libraries Selecting the 200th Ranked Item Number	Percent of Libraries Selecting
All (N=69)	48	69.5
75% (N=172)	128	74.4
50-75% (N=200)	147	73.5
25-50% (N=360)	242	67.2
10-25% (N=263)	129	49.0
Under 10% (N=149)	59	39.6

3. Type of library-ranking of the 200 most frequently selected item numbers

Several broad categories of types of libraries were established, and item number selections were then ranked by each of those types. Table 8-5 reports the results at the 200th benchmark ranking for each type of library. This table represents a summary of the rankings for each type of library and is presented in this fashion to facilitate a comparison of the consensus observed to exist among the several types of libraries. A comparatively higher consensus exists among public and academic libraries at the 200th most frequently selected item number than for the other types of libraries. On the other hand, a sharply lower consensus exists among law libraries at this level. Some possible explanations for this might be the fact that law libraries differ considerably in nature in that some are adjacent to another depository on a college or university campus whereas others are independent. Also, some of the law libraries might already have had subscriptions to the series when designated as law libraries and had not yet initiated a request through the depository system. In any case the differences which can be observed as a result of this comparison suggests that further examination is necessary.

4. Depositories by percent of item numbers received-ranking of the most frequently selected item numbers.

At present, our only indicator of the relative size of libraries is question 15 from the Biennial Survey. This question asks each library to indicate the percentage of depository items received; the results are tabulated in six categories. By ranking the most frequently received 200 item numbers for each of these six categories, it is evident, from Table 8-6, that a substantially greater consensus exists among large than among small libraries in the selection of item number categories. This finding might change if libraries are grouped in more homogenous groupings in each size range.

The findings reported in the tables presented in this chapter indicate that differences exist from one type of library to another. Even though the data are preliminary, some rather interesting questions can be raised. Once more background information on the libraries has been added to the computer file, we can further analyze patterns of document selection by item number. Our next step is to go beyond the 200 most frequently selected item numbers and look at the entire spectrum of item numbers. Categorization can also extend to the type of publication which item numbers represent (e.g., consumer).

5. Cross tabulation of selected factors which relate to collection development.

As already noted, the Biennial Survey included questions with collection development implications. For the purposes of this chapter, we cross-tabulated several questions, but will report here only two examples.

The first question, which asked if the libraries had a program for informing other libraries in their area of service of publications available through the depository, was cross-tabulated with the size of the depository collection in order to determine if size was associated with the tendency to share information about resources and services. Table 8-7 reports the cross tabulation and indicates that there is an association between these two factors. The libraries which indicate they receive all depository items are about evenly divided as to their activities for informing other area libraries of their services and publications. On the other hand, barely over 20 percent of those libraries which receive fewer than 10 percent of the depository items carry out this type of public information activity. For example, law libraries might receive fewer than 10 percent of the depository items and might not engage as actively in informing other libraries of their services and publications as do some of the other types listed.

The second question from the Biennial Survey asked if depository library selection provides sufficient coverage of government publications to handle the documents needs of the library's users. This, too, was cross-tabulated with the variable which indicates the size of the collection. The results of this cross-tabulation are reported in Table 8-8.

For some large libraries, depository selection is not large enough, but for the vast majority of libraries which receive a limited selection of depository items, the selection is adequate. The table shows a clear

Table 8-7: Do You Have a Program for Informing Other Libraries in Your Area of Services and Publications Available through the Depository Library?

Libraries by Percent Item Nos. Selected	Percent YES	Percent NO
All	50.75	49.25
75%	40.52	59.48
50-75%	43.85	56.15
25-50%	39.47	60.53
10-25%	39.83	60.17
Under 10%	21.90	78.10

Table 8-8: Does the Depository Selection Provide Sufficient Coverage of Government Publications to Handle the Document Needs of Your Users?

Libraries by Percent Item Numbers Selected	Percent Yes	Percent No
All	62.9	37.10
75%	70.18	29.82
50-75%	87.17	12.83
25-50%	92.28	7.72
10-25%	94.24	5.76
Under 10%	92.27	7.73

131

relationship between the percent of item numbers selected and the extent to which the depository selection meets the needs of the library's users.

Conclusion

The purpose of presenting the data reported in the tables is to indicate how the authors plan to use the Item Number File and the Biennial Survey File as sources of information about depository library collection development practices. The nature of the two files has been described as well as how we plan to use the files for a study of depository selection patterns. Information about the most commonly acquired item number series can be reported by various subsets of the depository library universe. In addition, the relationship between selected factors related to collection development can be reported.

This investigation into selection patterns of depository libraries has received the full cooperation of the U.S. Government Printing Office, and it provides one indication that the GPO is interested in advancing knowledge about document selection and retention by libraries. To be most effective, this type of study needs periodic replication so that subsequent data can be compared to those generated for this preliminary study. Such studies are of value to: (1) the GPO in keeping its distribution program and depository system attuned to the needs of partial depositories and their users, (2) partial depositories in the selection and retention of item number categories most needed by their clientele, and (3) non-depository libraries in knowing which item numbers are most frequently selected.

Item numbers reflect the archival heritage of the Superintendent of Documents Classification Scheme and do *not* provide a subject orientation. This weakness complicates research into collection development, especially for studies which attempt to adopt a structure of literatures approach. Without a subject orientation, one can question the value of the insights gained from examination of the item number file and the comparison of those item numbers selected to various variables.

The National Technical Information Service has a subject orientation to its resources. Consequently collection development is more easily studied for the publications of an agency which emphasizes informational matter than for one having an archival heritage of government documents as public records. The creation of a generally accepted subject/discipline scheme on the item numbers should be a primary objective of the Depository Library Council to the Public Printer as well as the various documents organizations. The purpose should be to determine which item numbers are pertinent to such disciplines as political science and sociology.

The authors of this chapter are currently working on a book related to collection development for government publications.[13] It will provide a more detailed analysis of the item number file, explore a subject model for the further examination of selections made by academic depository libraries, and probe social scientist use patterns. By employing various research methodologies, a more detailed understanding of the types and titles of federal government publications in greatest demand should emerge across institutional types (e.g., enabling such comparisons as academic institutions by highest degree offerings in combination with type of control, public or private). In this way, the authors can compare selection.to use and assist libraries in making retention decisions.

References

1. Adelaide Hasse, "Report of the Committee on Public Documents," *Library Journal*, 31 (August 1906): 140.

2. Bernard M. Fry, "Government Publications and the Library: Implications for Change," *Government Publications Review*, 4 (1977): 115.

3. For a more detailed discussion of collection development for government publications see: Peter Hernon, *Microforms and Government Information* (Westport, CT: Microform Review, 1981); and *Government Publications Review*, 8 (1981), Numbers 1 and 2.

4. Peter Hernon, *Use of Government Publications by Social Scientists* (Norwood, NJ: Ablex Publishing Co., 1979).

5. Ibid.

6. James C. Baughman, "Toward a Structural Approach to Collection Development," *College and Research Libraries*, 38 (May 1977): 241-248.

7. Kay Schlueter, "Selection of Government Documents in Law School Libraries," *Law Library Journal*, 71 (August 1978): 477-480.

8. For example, see Wilda B. Newman and Michlean J. Amir, "Report Literature: Selecting Versus Collecting," *Special Libraries*, 69 (November 1978): 415-424.

9. Kathleen T. Larson, "Establishing a New GPO Depository Documents Department in an Academic Law Library," *Law Library Journal*, 72 (Summer 1979): 484-496.

10. Fred W. Roper, "Selecting Federal Publications," *Special Libraries*, 65 (August 1974): 326-331.

11. Bruce Morton, "Toward a Comprehensive Collection Development Policy for Partial U.S. Depository Libraries," *Government Publications Review*, 7A (1980): 41-46.

12. Peter Hernon, "Functional Documents Collections," *Microform Review*, 9 (Fall 1980): 209-219; and Hernon, *Microforms and Government Information*.

13. Peter Hernon and Gary R. Purcell, *Collection Development for Government Publications* (Greenwich, CT: JAI Press, scheduled for publication in 1982).

GOVERNMENT DOCUMENTS IN SOCIAL SCIENCE LITERATURE: A PRELIMINARY REPORT OF CITATIONS FROM THE SOCIAL SCIENCES CITATION INDEX*

By Peter Hernon and Clayton A. Shepherd

Use patterns for government publications have been investigated through survey research, citation analysis, and analysis of sales records from one Government Printing Office bookstore.[1] A number of citation studies have included government publications as one category for analysis. The percentage of government publications cited in these studies has ranged from 2 to 36.[2] In some cases, government publications comprise a significant proportion of the total references cited, while in other studies they have not. Undoubtedly the source selected for investigation (e.g., periodical or index) accounts for this percentage difference. Some of these sources emphasize monographic and periodical literature, whereas others focus more extensively on government related activities and programs. For example, *International Organization*, a scholarly journal in the social sciences, yields a high percentage of government publications (24.8 percent).[3] After all, a "study of international organizations requires the use of documents as a primary source for research."[4] An investigation of *Social Sciences and Humanities Index*, on the other hand, produces a much smaller percentage of documents (2 percent).[5]

The differences among the citation studies do not help to clarify the role of government publications as an information resource for social scientists. The studies also do not draw upon a data base similar to the *Social*

*The authors wish to acknowledge the support by the Institute for Scientific Information, Philadelphia, Pennsylvania; the Emily Hollowell Research Fund, Simmons College; and Indiana University, where the computer analysis was performed.

Sciences Citation Index (SSCI). A study characterizing the government publications contained in this source by issuing agency and type (e.g., periodical and hearings) would add a new perspective on the use of government publications and thereby aid librarians in making broad selection and retention decisions. One caution, however, should be mentioned: social scientists use more government publications than they cite.[6] Consequently citation analysis provides only *one* indication of use; variations may occur on an institutional basis. Additional insights can be found from user and use surveys as well as an analysis of circulation records and actual reference questions asked.

Social Sciences Citation Index

This index, which began coverage with 1972, provides the footnotes and bibliographies from journals in various disciplines.[7] Realizing the importance of the *SSCI* to the social sciences, the authors, in 1978, contacted the Institute for Scientific Information (ISI) concerning a study of the government publications contained in one year of the index. As a result of the correspondence, ISI supplied three magnetic tapes (full reels at 1600 bpi) containing approximately 1.6 million records from the 1979 *SSCI*. The tapes were converted to CDC 6600 format in order to accommodate the computer at Indiana University, Bloomington.

The title of the cited journal for each entry is carried in a twenty character field and is often shown in the index exactly as represented by the authors of social science articles, who frequently—and inconsistently—abbreviate citations when they write for publication.[8] Also, since indexers at ISI must further shorten many citations to fit within the twenty character limit and do not operate from a controlled vocabulary; a given title may be listed in various ways. Furthermore, references do not indicate whether an item is or is not a government publication. Consequently the authors had to build a title and word search program that would scan the twenty character field and identify potential government publications. Once these entries were retrieved, the authors then had to examine the list manually in order to select those records which could definitely be identified as government publications.

Examination of the printed index for 1978 and 1979 indicated a variety of word and title search terms likely to yield government publications. Using these terms as search elements, four groups of 5,000 records were extracted and the initial search list expanded and refined on the basis of the 20,000 records examined. The title list eventually contained 57 full titles and their variations, while the word list had 115 individual words and their variations; Tables 9-1 and 9-2 provide a sample of the title and word search terms used.

The search programs were run and a printout of 129,060 citations was generated. These citations (as displayed in Figure 9-1) were checked

Figure 9-1: Raw Hit List Sample Printout

347475	INT J HLTH ED	19	1
347501	INT CATALOGING	6	7
347509	INT KATH Z	7	70
347543	INT REVIEW CONNECTIV	2	243
347553	INT LAW HISTORICAL P	5	298
347716	DEP STATE B MAR		27
347757	CDC768230 US DHEW PU		97
347792	WESTERN EUROPEAN ED	4	285
347806	PSYCHOL REP	31	851
347839	REPORT ACTIVE PLANNE		
347948	CARACTERE NATIONAL U		
348013	RP19560 LAB SPEC RAP		
348038	1ST INT C	2	
348052	ANNALS INTERNAL MED	77	169
348087	OCT C NAT CNRS STRAS	C	35
348147	J BONE JOINT SURG BR	52	757
348185	PICTORIAL ORG SHAPE		
348256	GENERAL COUNCIL M CO		
348285	P INT C SCI INFORMAT		
348293	OST15119 REP		
347476	INT J HLTH ED	19	3
347507	TEX REP BIOL MED S1	27	243
347511	HLTH SCI TV B	2	1
347551	J GEN PHYSIOL S	43	177
347571	PROGRESS MEDICAL GEN	4	128
347755	B ILLINOIS STATE LAB	10	1
347783	28TH EAAP ANN M		
347796	PSYCHOL REP	17	289
347832	ANN HUM GEN	38	243
347872	P INT COMPUTING S AC		555
348953	J NATL CANCER I	43	219
348014	ANN PEDIAT	24	263
348050	ANNALS INTERNAL MED	77	169
348062	ANNALS INTERNAL MED	89	550
348092	INT UNION CONSERVATI		115
348168	INT ANAESTHESIOL CLI	7	75
348249	8TH T INT C ROM FRON		253
348257	I PUBLIC ADM PUBLIC	7	
348289	UNESCO B LIBRARIES	15	126
348298	BLRD5390 REP		

Table 9-1: Partial List of Titles Used in the Search

```
FEDERAL REGISTER
FDA CONSUMER
FED RES BULL
FEDERAL RESERVE BULL
GAO REV
HISTORICAL STATISTIC
IMF SURV
INT LAB REV
INT LABOUR
INT LABOUR REV
MENTAL RETARDATION
MENTAL RETARDATION S
MO L REV
MON BUL STAT
MONTHLY B STATISTICS
MONTHLY LABOUR RE
MONTHLY LABOUR REVIEW
MONTHLY VITAL STA
MONTHLY VITAL STAT
```

Table 9-2: Partial List of Words Used in the Search

```
BUREAU              DEPT
CENSUS              DHEW
CENT                DIST
CIA                 DISTRICT
COAST               DIV
COLL                DWIGHT
COMM                EPA
COMMAND             ERDA
COMMISS             ERIC
CONG                  .
CONGRESS             .
CONGRESSIONAL        .
CORP
CORPS
COUNCIL
COURT
COURTS
CTR
DEP
```

manually and items identified as non-documents were deleted. Only 8,377 of these citations could be verified as possible government publications by the time of this conference (March 1981).[9] Since the authors are still examining this list, the number of actual documents may actually be less than this number. Incidentally the false drop rate from the search run was 93.5 percent.

Retrieval Rate

Of the approximately 1.6 million records in the data base, some 8,377 (0.5 percent) appear to be publications of the United States government and international organizations. This percentage is much smaller than that reported in the other citation studies and, therefore, represents a matter of concern to the authors. Publications distributed by the National Technical Information Service (NTIS) and the Educational Resources Information Center (ERIC) presented some difficulty in identification. NTIS publications, for example, might contain the "PB" or "AD" number without any reference to the clearinghouse.[10] The authors missed those ERIC publications only specifying the ED number, some abbreviations, misspellings (e.g., Unseco for Unesco), funded research projects which did not specify a government agency in the twenty character field, citations impossible to detect as government publications, and all references to the *International Social Science Journal*.[11] Still, given the 20,000 records examined on a sample basis, the authors believe that they have identified the majority of government titles appearing in the 1979 *SSCI*.

Examination of the *SSCI Journal of Citation Reports* for 1979[12] indicates that eight government titles have already been analyzed. Table 9-3 reflects variation as to the number of citations discovered for each title. For some reason, the authors uncovered only 3 percent of the citations to the *Federal Register* and 40 percent of the citations to the *Social Security Bulletin*. As well, they failed to recognize the *International Social Science Journal* as a government periodical. Representation of the other titles appears to be good; in fact, for *Federal Probation*, the authors had a better retrieval rate than did ISI.

In summary, except for the *International Social Science Journal*, the number of document titles retrieved from the data base appears to be satisfactory, although retrieval of all citations to specific titles reflects variations. Consequently, the authors plan to take another sample of records from the entire data base and to check them against the list of documents. This sample will, indeed, indicate how comprehensively document titles were identified, and might also suggest why the authors failed to identify all the citations to such titles as the *Federal Register* and the *Social Security Bulletin*.

Table 9-3: Government Periodicals Analyzed by ISI

Title	Number of Citations in Printed Index	Number of Citations* Extracted	% Extracted
Federal Probation	169	184	108.9
Federal Register	557	15	2.7
International Labour Review	184	154	83.7
International Social Science Journal	114	- - -	- - -
Monthly Labor Review	701	482	68.8
Problems in Communism	184	139	75.5
Social Security Bulletin	274	109	39.8
Unesco Bulletin for Libraries (now called Unesco Journal of Information Science, Librarianship and Archives Administration)	54	27	50.0

* These numbers are based on hand calculation and are, therefore, subject to error.

140

It should be remembered that this study should be labeled as a pilot project in which the authors have acquainted themselves with the pecularities of the data base and have delineated the methodology for a more extensive search for government publications in the entire *SSCI* data base, and that for the *Science Citation Index* as well. In this regard, it might be useful to review the study objectives.

Study Objectives

The objectives for this pilot study can be summarized as follows:

(1) to investigate the problems involved in studying the documents represented in the data base;
(2) to determine the extent to which government publications are contained in the data base;
(3) to examine patterns among the documents cited; and
(4) to identify topics for further investigation.

Under the third objective, the authors plan to investigate patterns as to: serial titles (what disciplines and journals cite documents, and what patterns exist as to the life span of a journal), issuing agencies (the identification of core agencies by disciplines), and level of government (the frequency of citations to U.S. government and international organizations), among other variables.

Not all of these objectives can be addressed in this article; final analysis must await completion of the study. The authors would also like to examine the amount of self-citation to a journal, the institutional affiliations of citing authors, and a variety of other topics. Such an analysis should indicate which document types and titles are more heavily cited by individual disciplines. It would also suggest, for example, which social science disciplines are most likely to cite publications distributed by NTIS.

Preliminary Findings

Except for the information taken from Volume 6 of the printed index, the following data have been hand calculated and, therefore, should be regarded as only an approximation. Computer statistical analysis has not yet been performed; at this time, greater attention has been placed on the identification of government publications in the data base.

Of the approximately 8,377 documents discovered, some 357 are ERIC distributed publications and 1,338 are publications of the National Academy of Sciences. In addition, there are 397 public health reports. Together, these three types of publications account for 25 percent of the identifiable government publications. The importance of the public health reports and the publications of the National Academy of Sciences undoubtedly reflects the overlap between this data base and the one for the *Science Citation Index*. Readers, therefore, should be cautious in their interpretation of government publications in the *SSCI* as characteristic of documents use by specific disciplines. To repeat, citation analysis provides only one element in constructing a profile of use patterns.

Eight periodical titles, as shown in Table 9-4, account for 24 percent of the remaining government publications. If the staff papers of the International Monetary Fund (2.1 percent) are added to this total, the percentage becomes 26. Frequently mentioned departments and agencies of the U.S. government included: Department of Agriculture; Department of Health, Education, and Welfare; Environmental Protection Agency; Federal Reserve Board; Geological Survey; National Aeronautics and Space Administration; National Bureau of Standards; National Museum; and the Smithsonian Institution. As for international organizations, there were frequent references to the United Nations itself, the Food and Agriculture Organization, International Monetary Fund, and United Nations Educational Scientific and Cultural Organization.

As mentioned earlier, the data base can be used to identify citation patterns to individual titles and to determine the life span of a journal. For example, Table 9-5 depicts the half-life (the number of journal publication years counting back from 1979 where the articles have accounted for 50 percent of the total identifiable citations) for seven titles analyzed in Volume 6 of the printed index. The *Federal Register* has the shortest life span and *Federal Probation* the longest. There may even be variations on an institutional basis. Still, the data depicted in the table suggest that such agencies as the U.S. Government Printing Office should not adopt a uniform five-year retention policy, but, instead, should provide for flexibility according to document type and title.

Table 9-6 provides additional insight into the citation patterns for the seven titles. Three-fourths of the citations to the *Federal Register* are to items published between 1972 and 1979. Combining the chronological distribution of citation counts with other information, librarians could well make decisions regarding retention, considering, for example, either retiring the pre-1970 volumes of *Problems in Communism* to subordinate shelf-space or discarding them. The entire run spanning the decade of the 1970s, or part of it, could then be made available in a microformat. Since this periodical began publication in 1952, selective holdings combined with an active weeding program would free a large amount of shelf space and still effectively address the majority of user requests.

The seven periodicals analyzed in the printed index can also be examined on the basis of which periodicals cite them. This information can be

Table 9-4: Serial Titles in the Data Base

Title	%
Monthly Labor Review	7.2
Journal of the National Cancer Institute	4.9
Federal Probation	2.7
International Labour Review	2.3
Problems in Communism	2.1
WHO Bulletin	2.0
Social Security Bulletin	1.6
Department of State Bulletin	1.1
Total:	23.9

Table 9-5: Rate of Obsolescence for Selected Periodicals

Title	Years
Federal Register	3.3
Social Security Bulletin	3.4
Problems in Communism	3.6
Monthly Labor Review	4.9
International Labour Review	6.1
International Social Science Journal	6.8
Federal Probation	8.7

Table 9-6: Cumulative Percentage of Citations from 1979 Journals to Articles Published during the Years*

	1979	1978	1977	1976	1975	1974	1973	1972	1971	1970
Federal Probation	0.00	5.91	10.05	17.75	23.66	33.72	41.41	45.56	51.47	54.44
Federal Register	10.41	32.67	47.75	54.39	60.50	66.06	72.34	75.93	78.81	80.78
International Labour Review	4.89	14.67	20.65	33.15	40.21	48.21	59.78	65.21	71.19	76.08
International Social Science Journal	0.00	4.38	11.40	28.06	37.77	44.73	50.87	56.13	61.40	68.42
Monthly Labor Review	5.42	23.10	35.66	42.93	50.49	59.76	65.76	69.18	72.46	75.17
Problems in Communism	7.06	20.10	40.76	54.34	64.12	73.91	79.34	83.69	88.03	89.67
Social Security Bulletin	1.82	21.89	37.95	62.77	68.97	71.89	77.73	86.49	87.95	89.41

*The data have been drawn from SSCI Journal Citation Reports (Social Sciences Citation Index). Volume 6, 1979 Annual. Philadelphia, PA: Institute for Scientific Information, 1980.

useful in determining core collections by discipline. The *Monthly Labor Review*, for example, is cited in such disciplines as law, economics and business, social work, history, sociology, and public policy. Table 9-7 reflects the distribution for half of this periodical's citations.

Table 9-7: Some of the Journals Carrying Citations to the *Monthly Labor Review* (percentages are based on the 701 citations from the printed index)

	%
Self-Citation	31.1
Urban Lawyer	3.3
International Journal of Social Economics	1.8
Aging and Work	1.6
Journal of Human Resources	1.6
American Journal of Economics and Sociology	1.4
Industrial and Labor Relations Review	1.4
Industrial Relations	1.3
Iowa Law Review	1.3
Modern Language Review	1.3
American Journal of Community Psychology	1.1
Journal of Employment Counseling	1.1
Social Problems	1.1
Wisconsin Law Review	1.1
Total:	50.5

Table 9-8 depicts a few of the disciplines from which other periodical titles are cited. The *Federal Register*, for example, is cited primarily by law journals. It is, however, also cited in such periodicals as the *Journal of Food Science*, *Journal of Taxation*, *Environmental Science and Technology*, and *Journalism Quarterly*. Together, these four titles accounted for 3.2 percent of all the citations to the *Federal Register*.

Conclusion

This article, which discusses research in progress, reflects some of the problems encountered in conducting a citation analysis and presents

Table 9-8: Five Government Periodicals and Selected Disciplines from Which They Are Cited

Title	Disciplines
Federal Probation	Criminal Justice, Law, Social Psychology, and Sociology
Federal Register	Law
International Social Science Journal	Sociology
Problems in Communism	Economics, Geography, and Political Science
Social Security Bulletin	Economics, Health Care and Medicine, Law, Public Policy, and Social Work

preliminary findings. Although these findings are tentative, they underscore the value of the information reported in Volume 6 of the annual printed index. Anyone interested in the application of collection development to government publications should monitor the cumulated data presented in the annual index.

Indexers at the Institute for Scientific Information work from the open literature and reduce titles of cited journals to a twenty character field. Certainly, changing the indexing pattern would be costly and would thus affect the cost of the printed index. The authors are not advocating such changes; however, they believe that others should be aware of the complexities in doing a citation analysis of this type.

Obviously, additional investigations of the government publications represented in the *SSCI*, and perhaps the *Science Citation Index*, are needed. These studies might determine, for instance, whether government publications are more likely to be cited if they have first been reported in the open literature. According to previous research, social scientists gather many of their references from the literature of their discipline, in particular from the monographic and periodical literature. A future investigation might survey those social scientists citing government publications and explore the methods by which they become aware of and acquire government publications. Perhaps they most often cite government publications from their personal collections.[13] Finally, the authors discovered an interesting fact while conducting their investigation. A number of social scientists who cite dissertations reference *Dissertation Abstracts International* and not the dissertation itself. It is our intention to study this finding and to write a separate paper on it.

References

1. Terry L. Weech, "The Use of Government Publications: A Selected Review of the Literature," *Government Publications Review*, 5 (1978): 177-184; Robert Goehlert, "A Citation Analysis of International Organization: The Use of Government Documents," *Government Publications Review*, 6 (1979): 185-193; Peter Hernon, "Use of GPO Bookstores," *Government Publications Review*, 7A (1980): 283-299; and Peter Hernon, *Use of Government Publications by Social Scientists* (Norwood, N.J.: Ablex Publishing Corp., 1979).

2. Weech, "The Use of Government Publications;" Goehlert, "A Citation Analysis of International Organization;" James C. Baughman, "A Structural Analysis of the Literature of Sociology," *The Library Quarterly*, 44 (October 1974): 296; Paula Mochida, "Citation Survey of Education Literature," *Hawaii Library Association Journal*, 33 (1976): 29-42; and June L. Stewart, "The Literature of Politics: A Citation Analysis," *International Library Review*, 2 (1970): 329-353.

3. Goehlert, "A Citation Analysis of International Organization."

4. Ibid., p. 185.

5. Baughman, "A Structural Analysis of the Literature of Sociology."

6. Hernon, *Use of Government Publications by Social Scientists*.

7. Items in *SSCI* are taken from journals in the fields of anthropology; archaeology; area studies; business, finance, management, and marketing; communication; community health; criminology and penology; demography; economics; education; ethnic group studies; geography; history; international relations; law; library and information science; linguistics; philosophy; political science; psychology; sociology; statistics; and urban planning and development.

8. It is interesting to note that Basefsky compared eight well-known style manuals and their treatment of government publications. He found a lack of general agreement: there is no clear way to cite authored and unauthored documents. Stueart Mark Basefsky, "Bibliographic Citations and U.S. Government Publications: A Conceptual Analysis and Comparison of Style Manuals" (MSLS thesis, University of North Carolina, 1979).

9. The authors could not hope to retrieve *all* the government publications contained in the 1979 data base. They had wanted to retrieve publications from the federal, state and local levels of government, as well as from international organizations. Examination, however, of the printed indexes, the first 20,000 records from the magnetic tapes, and selective inclusion of key terms in the word search list did not yield a significant proportion of state and local publications. Consequently they were deleted from the study, allowing it, therefore, to concentrate on the U.S. government and international organizations.

10. NTIS and ERIC serve as clearinghouses and provide access to government and contracted reports. Not all of the publications distributed, however, can be labeled as government publications. The authors do not plan to separate those which are documents from those which are not.

11. Determination of the fact that an item is, indeed, a government publication from the twenty character field is difficult. For example, one reference read "Federal Rules Eviden." By actually checking the periodical footnote, the authors discovered that this was a reference note to an appendix of Title 28, *United States*

Code. Also note that NTIS publications, for example, could be listed at least ten different ways. These include:

PB	US Nat Tech
PB	Nat Tech
Nat Tech In	
PB	Nat Tech Inf S
Nat Techn	
Nat Tech Info	
Nat Tech I	
NTIS	
US Nat Tech	
PB	rep

12. *SSCI Journal Citation Report (Social Sciences Citation Index).* Volume 6, 1979 Annual. Philadelphia, PA: Institute for Scientific Information, 1980.

13. Mary Ellen Soper, "Characteristics and Use of Personal Collections," *The Library Quarterly,* 46 (October 1976): 397-415.

BIBLIOGRAPHY

Articles

Baughman, James C. "A Structural Analysis of the Literature of Sociology," *The Library Quarterly*, 44 (October 1974): 293-308.

———. "Toward a Structural Approach to Collection Development," *College and Research Libraries*, 38 (May 1977): 241-248.

Buckley, Carper W. "Implementation of the Federal Depository Library Act of 1962," *Library Trends*, 15 (July 1966): 27-36.

Cohen, Diana B. "Unesco's Bibliographic Services," *International Library Review*, 9 (1977): 127-160.

Fry, Bernard M. "Government Publications and the Library: Implications for Change," *Government Publications Review*, 4 (1977): 111-117.

Goehlert, Robert. "A Citation Analysis of International Organization: The Use of Government Documents," *Government Publications Review*, 6 (1979): 185-193.

Hajnal, Peter I. "Collection Development: United Nations Material," *Government Publications Review*, 8A (1981): 89-109.

Hasse, Adelaide. "Report of the Committee on Public Documents," *Library Journal*, 31 (August 1906): 140.

Hernon, Peter. "Functional Documents Collections," *Microform Review*, 9 (Fall 1980): 283-299.

———. "Use of GPO Bookstores," *Government Publications Review*, 7A (1980): 283-299.

Hoduski, Bernadine E. "The Federal Depository Library System: What Is Its Basic Job?," *Drexel Library Quarterly*, 10 (January-April 1974): 107-122.

Inciardi, James A. "The Uniform Crime Reports: Some Consideration on Their Shortcomings and Utility," *Review of Public Data Use*, 6 (November 1978): 3-16.

Larson, Kathleen T. "Establishing a New GPO Depository Documents Department in an Academic Law Library," *Law Library Journal*, 72 (Summer 1979): 484-496.

Levine, James P. "The Potential for Crime Overreporting in Criminal Victimization Surveys," *Criminology*, 14 (November 1976): 307-330.

McClure, Charles R. "Microformatted Government Publications: Planning for the Future," *Government Publications Review*, 5 (1978): 511-515.

――――. "Opinion: GPO Inspection Program," *Government Publications Review*, 7 (1980): 450-452.

――――. "The Planning Process: Strategies for Action," *College and Research Libraries*, 39 (November 1978): 456-466.

――――. "From Public Library Standards to Development of Statewide Levels of Adequacy," *Library Research*, 2 (1980): 45-46.

Mick, Colin K. "Cost Analysis of Information Systems and Services," in Martha E. Williams, ed., *Annual Review of Information Science and Technology*, Vol. 14. White Plains, N.Y.: Knowledge Industries, 1979, pp. 36-64.

Mitchell, Daniel J.B. "Does the CPI Exaggerate or Understate Inflation?," *Monthly Labor Review*, 103 (May 1980): 31-33.

Mochida, Paula. "Citation Survey of Education Literature," *Hawaii Library Association Journal*, 33 (1976): 29-42.

Morton, Bruce. "Toward a Comprehensive Collection Development Policy for Partial U.S. Depository Libraries," *Government Publications Review*, 7A (1980): 41-46.

Newman, Wilda B. and Michlean J. Amir, "Report Literature: Selecting Versus Collecting," *Special Libraries*, 69 (November 1978): 415-424.

"A Plan for Collecting Oil and Natural Gas Reserves Data," *Statistical Reporter*, 77 (March 1977): 190-196.

"President Carter's Message on Libraries and Information," *Library Journal*. 105 (November 1, 1980): 2278-2279.

"Resolution on Unesco Publications," *Documents to the People*, 7 (September 1979): 213.

Reynolds, Catharine J. "Standards for Depository Libraries: Goals and Roadblocks," *Documents to the People*, 4 (March 1976): 45-46.

Richardson, John V., Dennis C.W. Frisch, and Catherine Hall. "Bibliographic Organization of the U.S. Federal Depository Collections," *Government Publications Review*, 7A (1980): 463-480.

Robinson, W.C. "Evaluation of the Government Documents Collection: An Introduction and Overview," *Government Publications Review*, 8A (1981): 111-125.

Roper, Fred W. "Selecting Federal Publications," *Special Libraries*, 65 (August 1974): 326-331.

Schlueter, Kay. "Selection of Government Documents in Law School Libraries," *Law Library Journal*, 71 (August 1978): 477-480.

Schrader, Alvin M. "Performance Measures for Public Libraries: Refinements in Methodology and Reporting," *Library Research*, 2 (1980-81): 129-155.

Schwarzkopf, LeRoy C. "The Depository Library Program and Access by the Public to Official Publications of the United States Government," *Government Publications Review*, 5 (1978): 154.

———. "Title 44 Revision," *Documents to the People*, 8 (September 1980): 228-230.

Shiskin, Julius. "Employment and Unemployment: The Doughnut or the Hole," *Monthly Labor Review*, 99 (February 1976): 3-10.

Skogan, Wesley G. "Measurement Problems in Official and Survey Crime Rates," *Journal of Criminal Justice*, 3 (Spring 1975): 17-31.

Soper, Mary Ellen. "Characteristics and Use of Personal Collections," *The Library Quarterly*, 46 (October 1976): 397-415.

Stewart, June L. "The Literature of Politics: A Citation Analysis," *International Library Review*, 2 (1970): 329-353.

"The Talk of the Town: the Librarian of Congress," *New Yorker*, (January 5, 1981): p. 24.

Weech, Terry L. "The Use of Government Publications: A Selected Review of the Literature," *Government Publications Review*, 5 (1978): 177-184.

Whitbeck, George W., Peter Hernon, and John Richardson Jr. "The Federal Depository Library System: A Descriptive Analysis," *Government Publications Review*, 5 (1978): 253-267.

Williams, J.G. "Performance Criteria and Evaluation for a Library Resource Sharing Network," in *Library Resource Sharing*. New York: Marcel Dekker, 1977, pp. 225-277.

Books

Bell, Daniel. *The Coming of the Post-Industrial Society*. New York: Basic Books, 1973.

Butler, Pierce. *Introduction to Library Science*. Chicago: University of Chicago Press, 1961.

Cherns, J.J. *Official Publishing: An Overview*. Oxford, England: Pergamon, 1979.

Churchman, C. West. *The Systems Approach*. New York: Dell, 1966.

———. *The Systems Approach and Its Enemies*. New York: Basic Books, 1979.

DeProspo, Ernest R., Ellen Altman, and Kenneth E. Beasley. *Performance Measures for Public Libraries*. Chicago: ALA, 1973.

Drucker, Peter. *Technology, Management and Society*. New York: Harper and Row, 1973.

Dubin, Robert. *Theory Building*. New York: The Free Press, 1969.

Hernon, Peter. *Microforms and Government Information*. Westport, CT: Microform Review, 1981.

———. *Use of Government Publications by Social Scientists*. Norwood, N.J.: Ablex Publishing Corp., 1979.

——— and Gary R. Purcell. *Collection Development for Government Publications*. Greenwich, CT: JAI Press, forthcoming.

Hoggart, Richard. *An Idea and Its Servants: Unesco from Within*. London: Chatto & Windus, 1978.

Kaplan, Abraham. *The Conduct of Inquiry: Methodology for Behavioral Science*. Scranton, PA: Chandler Publishing Co., 1964.

Lancaster, F. Wilfred. *The Measurement and Evaluation of Library Services*. Washington, D.C.: Information Resources Press, 1977.

Maheu, René. *La Civilisation de L'universel*. Paris: Laffont-Gonthier, 1966.

Marulli, Luciana. *Documentation of the United Nations System*. Metuchen, N.J.: Scarecrow, 1979.

Many Voices, One World: Report by the International Commission for the Study of Communication Problems. London: Kogan Page; New York: Unipub; Paris: Unesco, n.d.

Mialaret, Gaston, ed. *The Child's Right to Education*. Paris: Unesco, 1979.

Morehead, Joe. *Introduction to United States Public Documents*. 2nd ed. Littleton, CO: Libraries Unlimited, 1978.

Perkins, David L., ed. *Guidelines for Collection Development*. Chicago: ALA, 1979.

Rouse, William B. and Sandra H. Rouse. *Management of Library Networks*. New York: Wiley, 1980.

Sewell, James P. *Unesco and World Politics*. Princeton: Princeton University Press, 1975.

Sobakin, Vadim. *Unesco: Problems and Perspectives*. Moscow: Novosti, 1972.

SSCI Journal Citation Report (Social Sciences Citation Index). Volume 6, 1979 Annual. Philadelphia, PA: Institute for Scientific Information, 1980.

Stueart, Robert D. and George Miller, eds. *Collection Development in Libraries: A Treatise*. Greenwich, CT: JAI Press, 1980.

Toffler, Alvin. *Future Shock*. New York: Random House, 1970.

Unesco: What It Is, What It Does, How It Works. Paris: Unesco, 1980.

Eric Documents

Schwarzkopf, LeRoy C. "Regional Libraries and the Depository Library Act of 1962 (ED 066 177)

Government Publications

United States

Guidelines for the Depository Library System. Washington, D.C.: GPO, 1977.

Instructions to Depository Libraries. Washington: GPO, 1977.

U.S. Bureau of Labor Statistics. *The Consumer Price Index: Concepts and Content Over the Years*. BLS Report 517. Washington: Bureau of Labor Statistics, 1978.

U.S. Congress. House. Committee on House Administration. Subcommittee on Printing. *The National Publications Act*. Hearings, 96th Congress, 1st Session on H.R. 5424. Washington: GPO, 1979.

———. ———. ———. *National Publications Act of 1979*. 96th Congress, 1st Session, H.R. 5424.

———. ———. ———. Permanent Select Committee on Intelligence. Subcommittee on Oversight. *Intelligence on the World Energy Future*. Committee Print. Washington: GPO, 1979.

———. ———. Joint Committee on Printing. *Federal Government Printing and Publishing: Policy Issues*. Report of the Ad Hoc Advisory Committee on Revision of Title 44. Committee Print, 1979.

——. ——. Senate. Committee on Interior and Insular Affairs. *The Energy Information Act.* Hearings, 94th Cong., 2d. Session. Washington: GPO, 1977.

U.S. Government Manual 1980-1981. Washington: GPO, 1980.

U.S. President's Commission on Federal Statistics. *Report of the President's Commission.* Volumes I and II. Washington: GPO, 1971.

United Nations

United Nations. Dag Hammarskjold Library. "Policy Govering Development of the Collections: Acquisition, Retention and Maintenance." 1971- . (Directive A/24 and Annexes. Unpublished.

——. Secretariat. *Instructions for Depository Libraries Receiving United Nations Material.* 9 January 1981. (UN doc.ST/LIB/13/Rev.4).

——. ——. *Principles Govering Depository Libraries.* 17 November 1975. (UN doc. ST/AI/189/Add. 11/Rev. 1 and Amend.1).

——. ——. *Principles Govering the Exchange of United Nations Documents and Publications.* 22 June 1971. (UN doc.ST/AI/189/Add.4).

——. ——. *United Nations Documentation: A Brief Guide.* January 1981. (UN doc.ST/LIB/34/Rev.1)/

Theses

Basefsky, Stueart Mark. "Bibliographic Citations and U.S. Government Publications: A Conceptual Analysis and Comparison of Style Manuals." MSLS thesis, University of North Carolina, 1979.

Unpublished Material

Cherns, J.J. "Intergovernmental Organisations as Publishers: A Critical Look." Paper submitted to the Second World Symposium on International Documentation, Brussels, 20-22 June 1980 (UNITAR/AIL/SYM.2/WP.I/3).

Schaaf, Robert. "International Documentation: Serving Users' Needs." Paper submitted to the Second World Symposium on International Documentation, Brussels, 20-22 June 1980.

CONTRIBUTORS

Peter Hernon, who received his Ph. D. degree from Indiana University, Bloomington, is Associate Professor at the Graduate School of Library and Information Science, Simmons College. His teaching and research interests relate to government publications, reference services, and the social sciences. He is Associate Editor of *Government Publications Review* and has written extensively in the documents field, particularly on topics relating to reference services and collection development. Two of his books are *Use of Government Publications by Social Scientists* (Norwood, N.J.: Ablex Publishing Corp., 1979) and *Microforms and Government Information* (Westport, CT: Microform Review, Inc., 1981).

William J. Barrett is the Deputy Assistant Public Printer (Superintendent of Documents). Before joining the Government Printing Office in 1971, Mr. Barrett served as the Acting Administrative Officer of the Navy and capped a 23-year civilian career with Navy as a Staff Assistant to the Secretary of the Navy. Mr. Barrett was appointed by the Public Printer as the GPO member of the Interagency Council on Printing and Publications Services and serves as the Secretary of that body. Mr. Barrett has lectured at Harvard, Utah State University, University of Arizona, Syracuse University, South Dakota State University, University of Nevada, Rutgers University and State University of New York. He has addressed the annual meetings of the American Library Association, American Association of Law Libraries, Special Library Association, Federal Library Association, and Medical Library Association. Mr. Barrett's writings have appeared in the *Library Journal, Government Publications Review, Wilson Library Bulletin, Documents to the People,* and *Special Libraries.*

Bernard M. Fry is Director of the Research Center and Professor at the School of Library and Information Science, Indiana University, Bloomington. His documents related experience both within government and in academic institutions are as a college library administrator; head of Federal agency technical information services— and depositories—including the Atomic Energy Commission; the first director of the Clearinghouse for Federal Scientific and Technical Information (now the National Technical Information Service); grants administrator, National Science Foundation; and currently editor of the international journal *Government Publications Review* (Pergamon Press). Fry, who currently teaches courses on government documents and doctoral research, has published extensively in such areas as information science and government documents.

Peter I. Hajnal is Head of the Government Publications Section at the University of Toronto Library, Toronto, Canada. He holds an MS (LS) degree from Columbia University. His experience includes ten years' work at the Dag Hammarskjöld Library, United Nations, New York. His writings include one book, *Guide to United Nations Organization, Documentation and Publishing*, articles in *Government Publications Review* and *Journal of Library Automation*, and book reviews in *Unesco Bulletin for Libraries* and its successor. He has given lectures and participated in conferences and seminars on documents of international organizations. He is currently writing a book about Unesco and its publications.

Luciana Marulli-Koenig, Ph.D., Columbia University, 1979, has worked with United Nations documents for about ten years. An Italian citizen, she is the author of *United Nations Documentation: Bibliographic Control and Co-ordination* (Scarecrow Press, 1979), and of "International Documents Roundup", a column in *Documents to the People*. She has taught and lectured widely on international documentation. At present she is Bibliographer, Dag Hammarskjold Library, United Nations, New York.

Charles R. McClure currently is Associate Professor at the School of Library Science, University of Oklahoma. He has been head of the Government Documents Department at the University of Texas at El Paso Library and currently teaches courses in areas of government publications, administration, planning, and systems analysis. He serves as Assistant Editor for Federal Documents for *Government Publications Review* as well as being column editor for "Microformatted Government Publications." He has written extensively in areas of library administration and government publications including his recent book, *Information for Academic Library Decision Making* (Greenwood, 1980), and articles including, "Administrative Integration of Microformatted Government Publications," "Structural Analysis of the Depository Library System," "An Integrated Approach to Government Publications Collection Development," and "Indexing U.S. Government Publications." He is currently co-authoring a book with Peter Hernon entitled *Increasing Access to Government Documents Collections*, which should be available in 1983.

Joe Morehead is Associate Professor, School of Library and Information Science, State University of New York, Albany, New York. He is the author of *Introduction to United States Public Documents*, 2d ed. (Libraries Unlimited, Inc., 1978) and *Theory and Practice in Library Education: The Teaching-Learning Process* (Libraries Unlimited, Inc., 1980), as well as over 90 articles and 130 reviews in numerous periodicals. He was the first recipient of the ALA's 1977 Congressional Information Service, Documents to the People award.

Gary R. Purcell is Professor, Graduate School of Library and Information Science, University of Tennessee. He received his MLS from the University of Washington and Ph.D. in Library and Information Science from Case Western Reserve University. In addition he holds an MA in Political Science from Case Western Reserve. Dr. Purcell has taught courses in public documents at Western Michigan University and Case Western Reserve University as well as at the University of Tennessee. He has been the President of the Association of American Library Schools and the Tennessee Library Association. He has authored or co-authored several articles concerned with public documents and at present is collaborating with Dr. Peter Hernon of Simmons College in the preparation of a book concerned with collection development of public document collections.

LeRoy C. Schwarzkopf has been the regional depository librarian at the University of Maryland Libraries since 1967. He is a charter member of the Government Documents Round Table, American Library Association. He has made frequent contributions to *Documents to the People* since 1972 and has been Editor since 1978. He received a B.A. in History from Yale University in 1943, an M.A. in Education from the University of Michigan in 1951, and his M.L.S. from Rutgers University in 1967. He retired from the Army in 1966 after 20 years active duty as an Ammunition and Logistics Officer.

Clayton A. Shepherd is Associate Professor in the School of Library and Information Science at Indiana University, Bloomington campus. He received his AB and MA from the University of Maryland and did post-master's work at the University of Pennsylvania in the areas of sociology and criminology, and at the American University in the area of information management. He has been a Senior Systems Analyst at Sperry Univac, where he conducted research in the area of information retrieval and participated in the design and implementation of large-scale government information systems. In 1963 he was appointed Systems and Operations Manager for the American Society for Metals, where he assumed responsibility for the operation of its Metals Documentation Service. He is a Past President of the Indiana Chapter of the American Society for Information Science and in 1979 received that organization's Member of the Year award, and currently serves as its Student Chapter Advisor at Indiana University. He has published in the area of information science, and holds memberships in ASIS, the Association for Computing Machinery, the National Micrographics Association, and the Association of American Library Schools.